BLOOM & OTHER POEMS

T0270101

ALSO BY XI CHUAN

Available from New Directions

Notes on the Mosquito: Selected Poems

BLOOM & OTHER POEMS

Xi Chuan

TRANSLATED FROM THE CHINESE BY LUCAS KLEIN

A New Directions Paperbook Original

Manufactured in the United States of America
First published as a New Directions Paperbook (NDP1536) in 2022

Library of Congress Cataloging-in-Publication Data
Names: Xi, Chuan, 1963– author. | Klein, Lucas, translator. | Xi, Chuan, 1963– Bloom. | Xi, Chuan, 1963– Bloom. Chinese.
Title: Bloom : & other poems / Xi Chuan ; translated from the Chinese by Lucas Klein.
Other titles: Bloom (Compilation)
Description: First edition. | New York, NY : New Directions Publishing Corporation, 2022. | "A New Directions Paperbook Original" | Parallel text in English and Chinese.
Identifiers: LCCN 2022003357 | ISBN 9780811231374 (paperback)
Subjects: LCGFT: Poetry.
Classification: LCC PL2862.I1215 B56 2022 | DDC 895.11/52—dc23/eng/20220128
LC record available at https://lccn.loc.gov/2022003357

10 9 8 7 6 5 4 3 2 1

New Directions Books are published for James Laughlin
by New Directions Publishing Corporation
80 Eighth Avenue, New York 10011

ndbooks.com

Contents

Translator's Foreword   vii

Bloom   3
The One Who Happened   15
To Be Killed by a Cold   17
Awake in Nanjing   19
Trying to Talk About Flying without Clichés   33
Daily   35
What We Call   39
Abstruse Thoughts at the Panjiayuan Antiques Market   41
Eight Fragments   63
Annoyances   67
Travel Diary   73
Travels in Xichuan Province   85
Questions About the People   87
Stupid Words   89
January 2011 in Egypt   91
Random Manhattan Thoughts   101
Land Reclamation   113
Golden   115
On Reading   119
On the Noble   127
Don't Deprive Me of My Complexity   135
Ode to Facemasks   139
All Right, All Right   143
Loquaciousness, or: Thought Report   147
Mourning Problems   177
Inside   179

This Era Should Not Be Wasted:
  Xi Chuan in conversation with Xu Zhiyuan   181

Translator's Foreword

In the late 1990s a fierce debate broke out in the poetry community in China that divided poets into camps of "Intellectual" (知识分子) and "Populist" (民间) writers. As Maghiel van Crevel discusses in *Chinese Poetry in Times of Mind, Mayhem and Money*, the polemic corresponded to a series of binaries at play in attitudes toward art and literature in China, such as literary versus colloquial, sacred versus mundane, Westernized versus indigenous, mind versus body, and so on. To its critics, Intellectual writing was "elitist, artificial, alienated, and fake," whereas Populist writing was supposed to be "sensitive, honest, accessible and authentic, and belonging to ordinary people." Though the contentiousness of the debate has mostly faded, it nevertheless remains an important framework through which many poetry readers understand Chinese poetry today.

Xi Chuan, of course, was involved in the debate. He is one of the most prominent voices in contemporary Chinese poetry, and there can be no question that he is an intellectual, and his poetry Intellectual. In the interview at the end of this collection he explains that he thinks of himself as an artist, and in his poems you will find allusions to Inger Christensen, Roberto Bolaño, Bing Xin, Hegel, Rabelais, Guanyin (Avalokiteśvara), Xunzi, Ramesses II, among many other figures ancient and current; he has also recently published authoritative studies on the poetry of the Tang dynasty (618–907) and the painting of the Song dynasty (960–1279). Yet, while I want to avoid the cliché that he wears his erudition lightly, I do want to say that his erudition never comes off as pompous, dry, or pretentious, let alone elitist, alienated, or fake. Instead, knowledge and what Pound called "the dance of the intellect among words" appear in Xi Chuan's poetry as his poetry appears as a whole—warm, funny, charming, and inspiring.

Xi Chuan's published statements during this dispute were anti-binary: he pointed out that Populist poets played roles as public intellectuals and argued that the Intellectual's voice, though not the only voice, was an equally important one to be valued by the poetry reading-and-writing populace. This may seem like a common Intellectual deconstruction to avoid taking a side by arguing that the issue at hand is problematic in itself, but Xi Chuan's writing was also impacted by the polemic: he once told me that his sequence "A Sense of Reality," included in his previous collection in English *Notes on the Mosquito: Selected Poems*, was inspired by what he had learned from the Populist style ("Back no more than three generations, we laid offerings before the ancestral shrine in my home. / Back no more than three generations, I whiled away my time, playing cards or chess till dark"). The deconstructive critique of the stark separation of Intellectual from Populist writing also indicates an important aspect of Xi Chuan's poetics, that he simply does not see, and his poetry does not support, a separation of what is intellectual in literature from the emotional, affective, and human. The mind is *in* the body.

Bloom & Other Poems celebrates this convergence. The title poem is an exultation—an impassioned, sensual, intellectual romp. The most recent poems record his experiences with Covid-19; other poems, face mourning head-on. Even the most intellectually demanding poems, such as "Abstruse Thoughts at the Panjiayuan Antiques Market" and "Random Manhattan Thoughts," are both witty and grounded in everyday experiences. Such grounded knowledge and sensitivity are also on display in the interview that closes this volume (and which gained over seventy million views when it was broadcast on the internet in China). As he says in one poem, "Don't deprive me of my complexity!" And elsewhere, "I turned into five of me in 1992: the bitter me, the suspicious me, the uncertain me, the me who laughs out loud, and the me who navigates the cold and turbulent river of history." Like Whitman, like Pessoa, he contains multitudes.

I continued to translate Xi Chuan's poetry soon after *Notes on the Mosquito* was published in 2012. A small handful of the poems in this edition precede the publication of that volume, but the rest consist of recent work. This book thus represents the now of one of the most innovative and exciting poets of China, and the world, demonstrating how the intellectual and the emotional in poetry do not need to be at odds, but rather can be unified into a single, powerful poetic blooming.

I would like to thank Xi Chuan for reading every draft of my translations, as well as our editor Jeffrey Yang. For their support of the publication, we would like to acknowledge He Jiayu and Zhuang Xucheng, and for further help with the translations, my gratitude goes to Tammy Lai-Ming Ho, Chris Song, Forrest Gander, Richard Berengarten, and Eliot Weinberger, and of course to my wife, Shenxin Li.

—*Lucas Klein*

BLOOM & OTHER POEMS

开花

你若要开花就按照我的节奏来
一秒钟闭眼两秒钟呼吸三秒钟静默然后开出来

开花就是解放开花就是革命
一个宇宙的诞生不始于一次爆炸而始于一次花开

你若快乐就在清晨开呀开出隐着血管的花朵

你若忧愁就开放于傍晚因为落日鼓励放松和走神

或者就在忧愁里开放苦中作乐
就在沮丧和恐惧和胆怯里开放见缝插针

心有余悸时逆势开放你就释放出了你对另一个你的狂想

而假如你已开过花且不止一朵
你就退回青涩重新开放按照我的节奏来

我以滴水的节奏为节奏
因为水滴碰水滴这是江河的源头

再过分一点儿再过分一点儿水滴和水滴就能碰出汪洋大海

你得相信大海有一颗蓝色的心脏那庞大的花朵啊伟大的花朵

所以我命令你开花就是请求你开花
我低声下气地劝你

若你让我跪下我就跪下哪怕你是棵狗尾巴草

开出一朵梨花倘若你脖颈凉爽
开出一朵桃花倘若你后背因温暖的阳光而发痒

Bloom

if you're going to bloom then bloom to my rhythm
close your eyes for one second breathe for two be silent for three then bloom

to bloom is liberation to bloom is revolution
the universe did not begin with a bang but a bloom

if you're happy then bloom at dawn bloom a blossom hiding veins

if you're depressed then bloom in the evening because sunset promotes
    relaxation and absentmindedness

or in your depression bloom laughter to keep from crying
and in frustration and fear and timidity bloom wasting not and wanting not

bloom to counteract residual fear just release your fantasies of your
    other you

and if you've already bloomed in fact more than one blossom
then retreat to pre-ripeness and bloom again to my rhythm

my rhythm is the rhythm of dripping water
because water droplet hitting water droplet is the source of the river

to put it more extravagantly the deep blue sea comes from water droplet hitting
    water droplet

you must believe the sea has a blue heart oh such a great flower what a grand
    flower

so I order you to bloom that is request you to bloom
I humbly implore you

if you made me kneel I'd kneel even if you were foxtail bristlegrass

bloom a pear blossom in case the nape of your neck is cold
bloom a peach blossom in case your back is itchy from the warmth of the sun

但倘若你犹豫
倘若你犹豫该不该开花那就听我的听我的先探出一个花瓣来

然后探出两瓣然后探出四瓣

三瓣五瓣是大自然的几何

但你若愿意你就探出五十瓣五十万瓣这就叫盛开

而倘若你羞于盛开
你就躲在墙根里开放吧
开放到冰心奶奶告别她文艺青年多愁善感的小情调

而倘若你胆小
你就躲到篱笆后面开放吧
让陶渊明爷爷看到你就看到今天被狂人暴发户炸碎的南山

蚯蚓在等待

连苍蝇都变得更绿了更符合大地的想象了
连五音不全的燕子都歌唱了这使得王侯将相也有了心情不错的时候

他们在心情不错的时候也愿意珍惜他人的小命
甚至承认自己的命也是小命

而我要你开花
就是要你在心情糟糕的时候牢记小命也是命啊也是自然也是道

开花
用你的根茎发动大地深处的泉水

but in case you're still reluctant
in case you're still trying to decide whether to bloom or not to bloom then
        listen to me listen to me first stretch out a petal

then stretch out two petals then four petals

three petals and five petals are the geometry of nature

but if you want to you can stretch out fifty petals five hundred thousand petals
        is called a flourish

and in case you're too shy to flourish
then bloom hiding at the base of the wall
bloom till grandma Bing Xin parts with her hipster sentimentalisms

and if you're chicken
then bloom hiding behind a lattice fence
let grandpa Tao Yuanming see South Mountain strip mined by a maniac parvenu
        when seeing you

the earthworms are waiting

even the flies are growing greener to match the earth's imagination
even the tone-deaf swallows are singing this puts kings and marquises and
        generals ministers in a better mood

when they're in a better mood they care more about the lives of little people
they might even admit that they themselves are little people

but I want you to bloom
that is when you're in a rotten mood I still want you to keep in mind that little
        people are people they are natural they are the Dao

bloom
unleash a deep underground spring with your rhizome

在你和你的邻居闹别扭之后
在你和你的大叔小姨拍桌子瞪眼突然无所适从的时候

你就开花换个活法

老二老三老四脱了鞋子他们准备跳舞
老五老六老七眼冒金星他们准备嚎叫

开呀

尽管俗气地来吧尽管下流地来
按照我的节奏来你就会开出喜悦的花朵

有了喜悦你便不至只能截取诗意中最温和的部分
你便不至躲避你命中的大光亮

开花就是在深刻的静默之后开口说话呀呀说给另一朵深刻的花

不满意的人以为世界是个聋子
你扯嗓子谩骂不如开花
而开花就是让聋子和瞎子听见和看见

并且学习沉醉

开出野蛮的花开出让人受不了的花
开得邪门没道理没逻辑

像一百万平方公里的沙漠上大雨倾盆而下

开得异想天开倘若连天都开了那绝对是为了让你
恣意地开放

开到狂喜呀从死亡的山谷从废弃的村庄
从城市的地缝从中心广场

when you and your neighbor are having a falling-out
when you and your aunt or uncle pound the table and stare each other down and
        you don't know what to do

bloom and change your way of living

brothers two and three and four have taken off their shoes getting ready to dance
brothers five and six and seven are seeing stars getting ready to scream

go for it

even if it's vulgar even if it's obscene
do it to my rhythm and you'll bloom blossoms of happiness

with happiness you won't have to tear out only poetry's warmest parts
you won't have to shun brightness from your life

blooming is opening your mouth after a deep silence to whisper sweet nothings
        to another deep flower

unsatisfied people figure the whole world is deaf
but shouting obscenities isn't as good as blooming
while blooming is giving sight and sound to the deaf and blind

and learning how to be intoxicated

bloom barbaric blossoms bloom unbearable blossoms
bloom the deviant the unreasonable the illogical

like a heavy downpour on a million square kilometers of desert

bloom fantastical indulgence in case even fantasies bloom that would definitely
        be for you
to bloom with abandon

bloom till you're ecstatic from the valley of death from the village of rejection
from the crevasse of the city from the central square

中心广场上全是人呐
中心广场附近的胡同里全是沉默的牛羊

你去晚霞里逮一头羊吧分享它的好心肠
你去垃圾堆上逮一头猪吧摸摸它跳动的心脏

三千头猪个个鬓插花朵看谁敢把它们赶向屠宰场
九千只羊跳下山崖因为领头羊想死在山崖下面的花床上

开花呀孔子对颜回说
开花呀梁山伯对祝英台说

在三月在五月在雾霾的北京石家庄太原开封和洛阳
开花呀欧阳江河对他的新女友说

开出豹子盘卧树荫的姿态
开出老虎游荡于玻璃水泥和钢铁之林的大感想

开花是冒险的游戏
是幸福找到身体的开口黑暗的地下水找到出路

大狗小狗在二百五十个村庄里齐声吠叫就是你开花的时候

你开放
你就是勇敢的花朵勇敢在无聊打斗和奔窜里
你就是大慈大悲的花朵大慈大悲在房倒屋塌的灾难里

若石头不让你开放你就砸开它吧
它心房里定有小花一朵

the central square is full of people
the alleys around the central square are full of silent cows and sheep

go into the clouds at sunset and catch a cow or sheep share its good intentions
go into the dumpster and catch a pig touch its beating heart

three thousand pigs are wearing flowers in their bristles see who'd dare take them
    to the slaughterhouse
nine thousand sheep leap off a cliff because the lead sheep wanted to die in the
    flowerbed below

bloom said Confucius to Yan Hui
bloom said Liang Shanbo to Zhu Yingtai

in March in May in the smog of Beijing Shijiazhuang Taiyuan Kaifeng and
    Luoyang
bloom said Ouyang Jianghe to his new girlfriend

bloom the countenance of a panther curled up in the shade of a tree
bloom the contemplations of a tiger wandering through a forest of glass concrete
    and steel

blooming is a game of adventure
it's happiness finding the opening of the body dark underground water finding
    an escape

dogs of all sizes in two hundred and fifty villages bark in unison when you bloom

you bloom
you are a brave flower brave in your bored battles and scampering
you are a compassionate and merciful flower compassionate and merciful in
    catastrophes of crumbled buildings

if stones keep you from blooming then smash them open
there must be a small flower in the atriums of their hearts

若绳索不让你开放你就染红它吧
直到它僵硬然后绷断

你开呀你狠狠地开呀你轰隆隆地开

你开放我就坐起来站起来跳起来飞起来
我摇铃打鼓我大声喘气你也可以不按我的节奏来

你开到高空我就架张梯子扑上去

若你开得太高我就造架飞机飞上去

我要朗读你的呓语
我要见证你的乳头开花肚脐也开花脚趾也开花

我要闻到甚至吞噬你浩瀚的芳魂

我要跟你一起喊：幸福

是工地上汗毛孔的幸福集市上臭脚丫子的幸福
抽搐的瑟瑟发抖的幸福不幸福也幸福的他妈的大汗淋漓的幸福

所以你必须开花迎着我的絮叨

开一朵不够开三千朵
开三千朵不够开十万八千朵

开遍三千大千世界
将那些拒绝开花的畜生吊起来抽打

开花

if ropes keep you from blooming then dye them red
until they are so stiff they snap in half

bloom go ahead bloom cruelly bloom rumblingly

if you bloom I'll sit up stand up jump up fly up
I'll ring bells and bang drums I'll breathe loudly you can even do it without
     following my rhythm

bloom into the sky I'll climb up a ladder after you

if you bloom too high I'll build an airplane and fly after you

I want to recite what you say in your sleep
I want to witness your nipples blooming your belly button blooming your toes
     blooming

I want to smell to engulf the boundless fragrance of your soul

I want to shout with you: joy

the joy of pores on construction sites the joy of stinky feet in the open market
twitching trembling shivering joy unjoyful yet somehow still joyful joy dripping
     with fucking sweat joy

so you have to bloom to greet my loquacity

blooming once isn't enough bloom three thousand times
blooming three thousand times still isn't enough bloom one hundred eight
     thousand times

bloom three thousand boundless universes
and string up and beat any beast that refuses to bloom

bloom

当蚂蚁运送着甜就像风运送着种子
当高天行云运送着万吨大水就像黑暗中的猫头鹰运送着沉睡

群星望着你你也望着它们
你看不过来它们的闪烁就像它们看不过来你的丰盛

星宿一上修电脑的少年说开花
星宿二上骑鸵鸟的少年说开花

你听到了

月亮的背面有人开灯
哈雷彗星上有人噼啪鼓掌

开灯的人在乱七八糟的抽屉里找到他的万花筒
鼓掌的人一直鼓掌直到望见太空里灿烂旋转的曼陀罗

而你在花蕊的中央继续开呀
就像有人从头顶再生出一颗头颅

但倘若你犹豫
倘若你犹豫该不该开花那就听我的听我的先探出一个花瓣来

然后探出两瓣然后探出四瓣

三瓣五瓣是大自然的几何

但你若愿意你就探出五十瓣五十万瓣这就叫盛开

你就傻傻地开呀
你就大大咧咧地开呀开出你的奇迹来

2014.6.3

when ants distribute sweetness like the wind distributes seeds
when clouds soaring the skies distribute ten thousand tons of water like owls in
    darkness distributing sleep

the stars look at you and you're looking at the stars
you can't stand their twinkling like they can't stand your sumptuousness

the guy fixing computers on Alpha Hydrae says you should bloom
the kid riding an ostrich on Tau Hydrae says you should bloom

you hear it

someone turns on a light on the far side of the moon
on Halley's Comet people clap their hands

the man who turned on the light finds his kaleidoscope in a cluttered drawer
the people applauding applaud till they spot space's mandala spinning and
    shimmering

as you at the center of the stamen keep blooming
like someone growing another head from the top of her own head

but in case you're still reluctant
in case you're still trying to decide whether to bloom or not to bloom then listen
    to me listen to me first stretch out a petal

then stretch out two petals then four petals

three petals and five petals are the geometry of nature

but if you want to you can stretch out fifty petals five hundred thousand petals
    is called a flourish

just bloom like a fool
just bloom casually and carelessly come for all your marvelousness bloom

June 3, 2014

碰巧的人

他碰巧听说大地是方的，像他家中的方桌可用来吃饭和打牌。
他碰巧听说皇上是奉天承运的，而他只是老百姓这没什么。
他碰巧没听说过希特勒，这个留小胡子的人躲了他19年。
他碰巧没听说过文化大革命，他怀着正面的看法注视镜中的自己。

他来到北京，碰巧是晴天，没有雾霾；
他一鼓作气又去了内蒙，碰巧没赶上沙尘暴所以他不曾迷路。
蓝天白云的大草原使他确信远方确可向往，
他碰巧遇到一匹骏马允许他骑上一小时驰骋在天地之间。

回到家乡，他碰巧没遇上会计的女儿，就娶了水果批发商的女儿。
马路上，他碰巧避过了车祸，生命持续着就伟大。
他学驴叫出神入化很开心，没意识到这是中文的驴鸣。
他碰巧生为中国人，碰巧读过《红楼梦》没读过《巨人传》。

他碰巧认识杨树、柳树，不认识梧桐树。
他碰巧三次捡到钱包，如果有第四次，还会是碰巧吗？
他碰巧不了解"二"这个字的丰富内涵，邻居们知道但没告诉他。
他体会着二流的幸福，碰巧得到了春风的鼓励。

2014.8.19 / 2017.4.27

The One Who Happened

He happened to hear the world was square, like the square table at home that could
    be used for eating or playing cards on.
He happened to hear that the emperor is made so by divine right, but he's just a
    commoner so that's nothing.
He happened to have not heard of Hitler, that guy with a little mustache who
    avoided him for nineteen years.
He happened to have not heard of the Cultural Revolution, and looked at himself
    in the mirror in a positive light.

When he came to Beijing, it happened to be a clear day, no smog;
in a spurt of energy he went to Inner Mongolia, where he happened not to run
    into a sandstorm and so never got lost.
Convinced by the blue sky with white clouds above the grasslands that all distance
    was reachable,
he happened to meet a stallion that let him ride for one hour at full gallop
    between heaven and earth.

Back in his hometown, he happened to not run into the accountant's daughter,
    so he married the daughter of the fruit wholesaler instead.
On the street, he happened to avoid a car crash, and it was great that life could
    go on.
He learned how to bray just like a donkey, and was so happy he didn't notice it
    was a donkey braying in Chinese.
He happened to be born Chinese, happened to read *Dream of the Red Chamber*
    not *Gargantua and Pantagruel*.

He happened to know poplars and willows, but not the paulownia tree.
He happened to find a wallet three times, but if there were a fourth time would
    it still be that he *happened to*?
He happened not to know the rich connotations of the word *second*, and though
    his neighbors know they're not telling him.
He has experienced a second-rate happiness, and happened to be encouraged by
    the spring breeze.

August 19, 2014 / April 27, 2017

死于感冒的人

他不肯相信他会被几个小人所打倒。
他不怕蛇蝎猛兽——凶猛的它们已成陈词滥调。
这逆风而行的人：风愈大，他落脚迈步愈有力。
他本应倒在雷电之中，如悲剧剧本所述，以符合一个英雄的身份。

然而他倒下，出乎所有人意料。
他不肯相信，几个小人用小儿科的手段，
抖抖机灵，就将他打倒；他相信
在小人背后站着阴险而强大的敌人例如一种价值观化成的巨妖。

所有人都看见了，他是负有使命的人；
他自己更要求与其崇高的理想相对称的敌人。
多年以来他瞧不起市侩，
远离市侩，他断定历史会赏脸把他的意思弄明白。

从生活的全部滑稽中挤出了往往呈现于打架斗殴的严肃性。
你看他被几个小人所打倒，不可能啊。
这让错愕的蛇蝎猛兽们只好求助于陈词滥调：哎呀，哎呀。
仿佛他战胜了癌症，却死于感冒。谁也没有料到。

2007.8

The Man Who Was Killed by a Cold

He never believed he'd be beaten down by such petty figures.
He wasn't afraid of snakes or scorpions or beasts of prey—these vicious things had
    already become clichés.
This man who went against the wind: the stronger the wind, the stronger he'd
    plant his feet as he made his strides.
He was supposed to be struck down by lightning, as if written in a tragedy, in
    accordance with his heroic identity.

But when he fell, it was beyond everyone's expectations.
He couldn't believe it, these petty people with their elementary moves,
their trembling wits, striking him down; he believed
behind these petty figures must be some nemesis insidious and strong like a
    hobgoblin transmogrified from values.

Everyone saw it, he was a man on a mission;
he demanded a nemesis equal to his lofty ideals.
For so many years he had hated mercenaries,
but far from mercenaries, he concluded that history would have to honor him
    by getting his point.

Out of the comedy of life is squeezed the severity that so often appears in a fight.
You see him being beaten by such petty figures, and it doesn't even seem possible.
Even the dumbfounded snakes and scorpions and beasts of prey appeal to cliché
    for help: oh me, oh my!
As if he'd beaten cancer, only to be killed by a cold. No one saw it coming.

August 2007

醒在南京

天醒的一刻我闭着眼听见雨声呃呃呃是听了半生的雨声并不浪漫
雨声逼近夹着孤单的汽车声
汽车走远时雨声亦挪远但不一定是雨声挪远它只是变小
就像一个人的存在不一定消失只是重量变轻

想象雨点儿扑地雨伞和雨衣的风景湿润
静静的脚手架大吊车没有工人爬上爬下爬来爬去的一二三四五六个工地
店铺小老板寄望在这样的天气卖出雨伞和雨衣

奇怪
乡村的小雨淋在城市的大脑壳上
小雨中的杏花张望着窗畔喝茶的小文人这是我印象里的江南

这是地主秀才和农民的江南配合着书中自有黄金屋加颜如玉的古训
而今小老板和打工者的江南也是江南吗资本家的江南
肯定不是江南因为颜如玉不再投奔书本

怎么没有鸟鸣呢这是清晨的错还是鸟雀的错
不知道我在用盲人的耳朵搜寻吗
北京的鸟鸣开始于清晨四点而此地的鸟鸣几点开始是一个莎士比亚的问题

或者鸟雀已相约不再啼鸣
孟浩然死去约1300年了他为鸟鸣写下的诗句代替他活了约1300年
对美国人来说这时间够长了对埃及人来说这不算什么

孟浩然习惯于山清水秀的生活可以想见他长得也山清水秀
但无法想象他以何为生诗人又不代表生产力

Awake in Nanjing

the instant the sky wakes my eyes are shut I'm listening to the rainfall *huh huh*
    huh listening to half a lifetime of rainfall isn't romantic
the sound of rainfall approaching mixes with the sound of a solitary car
the car going away pushes the sound of rainfall away but maybe it's not pushed
    away so much as letting up
like someone's existence maybe it's not the person disappearing so much as
    lightening

imagine raindrops hitting the ground umbrellas raincoats scenery soaked
one two three four five six construction sites of silent scaffolding cranes no
    workers climbing up or down or all around
a bodega owner hopes umbrellas and raincoats will sell in weather like this

strange
light rain from the country falling on hard heads in the city
apricot blossoms in the light rain peeping through a window at a poetaster
    sipping tea this is my image of Jiangnan

this is the Jiangnan of the scholarly landlord and the peasant in concert with the
    maxim that houses of gold and jade-like faces are contained within books
but are the Jiangnan of the small business owner and the day laborer still Jiangnan
    the capitalist's Jiangnan
is definitely not Jiangnan since jade-like faces no longer seek shelter in books

why don't the birds sing is it the morning's fault or the birds' fault
don't they know I'm searching with ears of the blind
in Beijing the birds start singing at four a.m. but here what time do the birds
    start singing this is a Shakespearean question

or else the birds have agreed not to sing again
Meng Haoran died about 1300 years ago and for 1300 years the little poem he
    wrote about birds singing has lived in his stead
that's a long time for an American but won't impress an Egyptian

Meng Haoran was used to a life of sharp mountains and clear waters so we can
    infer how sharp and clear he looked
but we can't imagine how he could make a living poets never represented the forces
    of productivity

他偶尔向江水吐露胸中怨气不奇怪
他是否因此卓尔不群于草莽是否凭怨气结交到王维和李白
可王维李白从不互致问候当他们同在长安的时候他们互相瞧不起

大江流日夜啊大江流动在我的床边这样说太夸张了

我改口

大江流动在我南京或金陵或六朝古都的客栈门前
这是客栈或这是旅馆或这是宾馆或这是酒店
对电话里的朋友说这是酒店对自己说这是客栈

有啥不同吗古人只住客栈并在墙上题字
流风入民国方鸿渐将女人按倒在床时发现枕侧墙上题写的云雨
原来是昨日

女人女人秦淮河夜晚虽然依旧挂红灯但妖精的没有那里现在只卖小吃
干净的床铺四个白色的枕头我只用了两个
舒服的肉体舒服的勃起我在着昨天我不在前天我也不在

镜子里一个对称的房间有另一个我与我对称着你是我吗
电视机黑屏左下角小红灯亮着表明它有电像少先队一样时刻准备着
你用我吧
遥控板一按就是媒体的世界

我微睁开一只眼旋又闭上

it wasn't strange for him to get something off his chest from time to time and tell
    it to the river
is this why he stood apart from the crowd how trading up on his grievances he
    associated with Wang Wei and Li Bai
but Wang Wei and Li Bai never acknowledged each other when they were both
    in Chang'an they looked down on each other

the river flows on night and day oh the river flows by my bedside oh this is
    too much

I'll withdraw it

the river flows by the door of my inn in Nanjing or Jinling or the Ancient Capital
    of the Six Dynasties
this is an inn or this is a guesthouse or this is a hotel or this is a resort
to friends on the phone it's a resort it's an inn to me

what's the difference the ancients only lived in inns and wrote poems on walls
but in the Republican era Fang Hongjian got a girl in bed only to find a dirty
    ditty on the wall behind the pillow
written yesterday

girls girls though red lanterns are still raised over the river Qinhuai at nighttime
    there are no more seductress spirits just snackfood
on a clean white bed are four white pillows I use only two
body comfortable erection comfortable I'm in my yesterday not in now not in
    the day before yesterday

in the symmetrical room in the mirror is another me are you the me I'm
    symmetrical with
the red light in the left lower corner of the black TV screen is on to show the
    power is on like the Young Pioneers showing they're ready at any minute
use me
a press on the remote control and it's the world of media

I open an eye and then shut it

今天谁死啊谁晒裸照今天哪个地方的工厂会爆炸
今天哪个地方的城管要打人哪个地方的桥梁会垮塌哪个领导会被双规

七点二十分听见鸟鸣了鸟鸣来得忒晚我是身处深涧之中吗

分裂的现实感我内心的鸟鸣早已开始
我从未向人提起我内心的众鸟来自不远处的敬亭山
李白曾见敬亭山众鸟高飞尽但不知这众鸟是来到了我的心间喳喳叫个不停

它们分成十六个派别选择在我心里吵嘴
它们吵嘴时顾不上为旭日而歌唱

而窗外的鸟鸣尽量满足孟浩然的倾听
仿佛窗外的世界不是真正的世界只有出事的世界才是真正的世界
不出事的世界不让人相信它的真实性仿佛它是虚拟鲍德里亚也有说不准的时候

于是有人跳楼被路人伸手接住
伸手救人者被砸成高位截瘫被感动的市民响应报纸号召捐款捐物
而获救者拒绝捐出跳楼前夜的内心纠结
而获救者被惊吓的爹妈以为世界会就此平静

走廊里飘过人声地毯中的细菌将脚步声吃尽

who will die today whose nude photos released which factory explode
which police department will commit brutality today which bridge collapse
     which politician detained

at 7:20 I hear the birds singing that's incredibly late am I in some deep ravine

in the split sense of reality in my mind the birds started singing hours ago
I've never told anyone that the birds in my mind come from Jingting mountain
     not far from here
Li Bai saw the birds on Jingting mountain all fly away but never learned where
     those birds went they flew into my mind and won't stop chirping

they've divided into sixteen competing camps and decided to hash it out in my
     mind
hashing it out they don't care they're singing for the rising sun

while the birds singing outside do their best to satisfy Meng Haoran's eavesdropping
as if the world outside the window weren't the real world only the world where
     accidents happen is the real world
a world where accidents don't happen can't convince people of its reality like
     Baudrillard's simulacrum can be unsure sometimes

so someone who jumped off a roof was caught by someone on the street stretching
     his arms
the one who stretched his arms to save him was crushed into paraplegia the
     townspeople were so moved by the appeals in the newspaper they donated
     money and goods
and the one who'd been saved refused to make a donation the turmoil in his mind
     the night before he jumped
and the shocked parents of the one who was saved thought there'd be calm and
     peace in the world

sounds of people in the hallway the bacteria in the carpet eat up all the sounds
     of footsteps

七点二十五分
梦的残渣
小夏说泳池池水太冷所以她上岸穿了件衬衣复入水中
管理员又把她叫上岸来说不许穿衬衣下水如果觉得太冷可以穿三件泳衣

七点二十七分
梦的残渣
小冯听见有人敲门便问谁呀门外人粗声回答是我这究竟是坏人还是好人
小冯再问什么事呀门外的粗声回答是不一定

梦中事算不算往事呢
梦中事若不算往事为何往事总向梦中事看齐

听见厕所冲下水的声音我活着别人也活着
污水处理厂就近建在长江边上也许管百分之三十的用

但把尿直接撒到长江里的事我不干就像孟子吃肉而远庖厨
是有点儿虚伪是文明的必要的虚伪
如能躺在床上眺望长江我会虚伪而快乐地大声感谢合法的生活和非法的生活

客栈门外长江夜晚定有中华鲟游过但这是什么鱼呢
这么隆重的名字这么俗气的名字是谁给起的名字这是濒危物种吗
大熊猫何不叫中华熊

长江上的运沙船吃水很深油漆斑驳没有一艘是新的
迎着水面敞开奶子的女人前面抱后面抱都是女人的女人没有一位是难看的

at 7:25

the residue of a dream

Xia said the water in the pool was too cold so she got out put on a shirt and went
back in

the manager told her to get out he said you can't wear shirts in the pool if you're
cold you can put on three swimsuits

at 7:27

the residue of a dream

Feng hears someone knocking at the door asks who is it on the other side someone
says in a husky voice it's me well good guy or bad guy

Feng asks what is it and on the other side someone says in a husky voice I'm not
sure

is a dream the past

if a dream isn't the past why does the past try to keep up with dreams

I hear a toilet flush I'm alive others are alive too

the water treatment plant in the vicinity of the Yangtze might make a difference
of thirty percent

but to piss directly in the Yangtze I won't do that like Mencius ate meat but kept
clear of the kitchen

it's a little hypocritical it's the hypocrisy necessary for civilized behavior

if I can lie in bed looking at the Yangtze I will hypocritically and happily give
thanks to both legal life and illegal life

outside the inn at night there must be Chinese sturgeons swimming by in the
Yangtze but what kind of fish is this

such a grand name such a vulgar name who conferred it is it an endangered species

why isn't the giant panda called the Chinese bear

the sand barges on the Yangtze ride low in the water paint blotchy not a single boat
is new

the women baring their breasts to the water at stern and bow all women's women
not a single one ugly

杜十娘怒沉百宝箱
两岸俗丽的花朵没有一朵为此而绽放那些快活的灯火没有一盏为此而熄灭

滔滔江水东去也

去年我曾到此一游曾从建错了风格的阅江楼眺望大江
我假设我是龚贤一望大江开
我本假设我是高启登上雨花台眺望大江来从万山中但没能得逞

江水改了道从雨花台望不到明代的大江了

从我的床铺也望不到大江这意味着我不是康熙我也望不见天下
既望不见广州的人山人海也望不见重庆的人山人海
只好自认匹夫一个却又无干兴亡

读报读网络新闻关心天下大事顶个屁用啊读小说而已
我的小学老师中学老师害我不浅呐他们把我训练成一个旁观者
一棵旁观的桃树或李树连开花也不必了

城里的梧桐树被放倒了地产商在市政府里有朋友
我若当选下届市长我将把那些民国时代的梧桐树植回原处但无此可能

所以我不和他们交朋友
我不喝酒我爸也不喝酒我爷爷也不喝酒

Du Shiniang threw her treasure chest into the water in anger
of all the pretty flowers on the banks not one blooms because of this of all the
    cheery lanterns not one goes out because of it

thus eastward do the torrents of the river flow

last year I took a trip here and gazed at the river from the Yuejiang Tower it's
    reconstructed all wrong
I pretended I was the painter Gong Xian gazing at the openness of the river
I tried to pretend I was the poet Gao Qi ascending Rainflower Lookout to see
    the river emerge from ten thousand peaks but I couldn't get it right

the Yangtze changed its course from Rainflower Lookout you can't see the river
    as it was in the Ming dynasty

from my bed I can't see the river either which means I'm not Emperor Kangxi I
    can't see all under heaven
I can't see the teeming multitudes in Guangzhou I can't see the teeming
    multitudes in Chongqing
I may as well accept my fate as an ordinary man at least I have nothing to do
    with the rise and fall of the empire

reading the paper reading online news worrying about everything under heaven
    it doesn't do shit read short stories instead
my grammar school teachers my high school teachers they ruined me for life
    they trained me to be an observer
an observing peach or plum tree doesn't even need to blossom

the paulownia trees in the city have been felled the property developers have
    friends in city government
if I were elected the next mayor I'd have all the Republican era paulownias
    replanted back where they were but this is impossible

so I don't make those kinds of friends
I don't drink my dad doesn't drink my grandpa didn't drink

所以我能在七点三十分顺利地睁开双眼我幽暗的大脑就透进了光亮
我望着天花板它虽有欧洲的豪华风格却是石膏做的

那石膏峻岭似的财富巍峨到吓人可算个屁呀
昨天掉在我头上的三张小馅饼算个屁呀小小的声誉算个屁呀
工程师们的成就感来得太容易了工艺美术大师们的成就感来得更容易

假装不俗其实很俗的趣味算个屁呀中等才华算个屁呀但已经不容易了
但算个屁呀

权与势在韩非子看来顶顶重要可在庄子看来算个屁呀

清醒的大脑嗡嗡叫了灵魂也醒了

历史分可被理解的部分和不可被理解的部分哪部分更强大
精细的品味在一个粗糙的时代该怎样传播
传播精细的品味等于传播亡国的种子这可以北宋为例土豪们不吃这一套

哦不能明说的不满和不肯说出的抱怨

该下床洗个澡了睡乱的头发让人以为我夜夜噩梦其实不是
肚子上的肉该收一收了睡醒的口腔该被刷一下了
韩愈写落齿诗应在五十岁以前

七点三十五分谁给我上发条好让我关心一下我自己
昨晚不会关的灯只好让它亮到现在我确实关闭了所有的开关

so I can easily open my eyes at 7:30 my bleary brain just lets in the light
I look at the ceiling in luxurious European style but it's made of plaster

who gives a shit about mountains of plaster wealth so lofty it's scary
who gives a shit about the three beef patties that fell on my head yesterday who
    gives a shit about a modicum of fame
accomplishment comes too easily for engineers accomplishment comes too
    easily for masters of arts and crafts

who gives a shit about liking to pretend not to be so vulgar it's vulgar who gives
    a shit about average talent but even that isn't easy
but who gives a shit

power and influence were of supreme importance to Han Feizi but Zhuangzi
    didn't give a shit about them

my brain is wide awake buzzing for my soul to wake up

which is greater that which can be understood in history or that which cannot
    be understood
how can refined taste be propagated in a crass age
propagating refined taste means propagating the seeds of the collapse of the
    country take the Northern Song dynasty for example the new tycoons
    aren't buying it

ugh the discontent you can't speak freely and the complaints you won't make
    out loud

I should get up and shower bed head makes people think you have nightmares
    every night but that's not the case
I should lose some weight my teeth need brushing I have bad breath when I get
    up
Han Yu wrote a poem about losing his teeth it must have been before he turned fifty

at 7:35 who wound me up like a watch so I could take care of myself
last night I flipped every switch I couldn't figure out how to turn off one light
    so I left it on until now

昨晚的宴会余音还在
两个喝高到又搂又抱的男人两条被酒精加宽了的舌头
一个说我刚去过法兰克福看我的皮包另一个说我刚去过巴黎看我的皮鞋

他们说的是自助游哇跑一趟欧洲九天十国
孔夫子周游列国要能有这样的速度2500年前的天下就能免于礼崩乐坏
而跑步穿过欧洲说明欧洲没什么好看的
或者说明他们真真来自后发达国家只能玩得这么辛苦

还不如好好待在江南天天眺望大江
从不同的角度
康熙到来的时候一定兴师动众

端午将近
端午在任何国家都没有意义只在江南有意义而江南就是我床下这块土地
这也是吴地但也是楚地吗
我在楚国有朋友我在吴国没有朋友我在江南倒也有朋友而此刻我一个人

路漫漫其修远兮路边的客栈一家一家何其多也一直排到天尽头

我撩开被子下地双脚认进一次性纸拖鞋

深呼吸

站稳

2013.7.14–11.21

sounds from last night's banquet still linger
two men hugging each other they drank so much two tongues fattened by alcohol
one said I just went to Frankfurt look at my bag the other said I just went to
    Paris look at my shoes

they were talking about package tours to Europe whoa see ten countries in nine days
Confucius traveled through the central states if he had kept that pace there'd have
    been no degeneration of the rites under heaven 2500 years ago
but running through Europe just proves there's nothing to see there
or else proves they come from a recently developed country it's not easy for them
    to relax

why not just spend time in Jiangnan and watch the river flow everyday
from different angles
when emperor Kangxi came it must have been a real campaign

it's almost Dragon Boat Festival
Dragon Boat Festival doesn't mean anything in any country it only means
    something in Jiangnan and Jiangnan is this land beneath my bed
it was the kingdom of Wu but was it also the kingdom of Chu
I have friends from Chu I have no friends from Wu I do have some friends from
    Jiangnan but right now I'm on my own

how far into the distance stretch the roads inn after inn along this road reduplicating
    themselves to the end of the sky

I toss off the blanket slide my feet into two paper slippers

take a deep breath

and stand up

July 14–November 21, 2013

尽量不陈词滥调地说说飞翔

每回思欲飞翔　都感身体沉重
每回奋力起飞　顶多腾空五尺

然后坠地　露出本相

有回我高飞到九尺　瞬间心生苍茫
落地摔疼屁股　屁股大骂心脏

偶夜梦里悬空　由树梢跃升楼顶
由楼顶登脚而起　见半月在我左手

我浴三光即永光　我入黑暗遇无人

怀落寞而归床　上厕所而冲水

次日回味　一声不响
走路　被一男孩叫"爷爷"

问孙子"你叫啥"　回说"我叫飞翔"

2014.11.11

Trying to Talk About Flying without Clichés

every time I think of flying   my body feels heavy
every time I try to take off   I soar no higher than five feet

then fall to the ground   revealing my true self

one time I reached nine feet   my heart lifting to the boundless
but bruised my ass when I crashed down   and my ass cursed my heart

one night I dreamt of floating   from treetop to rooftop
and from rooftop ascending upward   half moon at my left hand

bathing in the eternal shine of the stars   entering darkness to meet no one

and then back to bed in solitude   then I went to the bathroom and flushed
    the toilet

thinking back the next day   without the echo of a sound
walking down the street   a boy called me *Grandpa*

What's your name, grandson? I asked   *My name is Flight*, he said

November 11, 2014

日常

说话的人忽然多起来不止在我的窗下
说话的人嗓门忽然大起来仿佛大声说话才不是沉默

*

脱鞋，想起在飞机上脱鞋的人
吃药，想起梦想永生的人

*

骂人，为了正义；有时只是为了出口恶气
为了一个美好的明天，有人建议禁止骂人。那怎么行？

*

打开电脑，网络信息多得像蝗虫
网络的无组织性竟然凑成历史。那谁负责遗忘呢？

*

而历史，只有被夸张才能被看见
而无法被看见的生活在重复中持续

*

过分地生活才是生活此外没有生活。有人反驳
过分的美才是美此外没有美。有人反驳

*

过分的愚蠢被围观，被赞美，被打听
终得以幸免变成一个笑话。反驳者随大溜地笑了

Daily

Suddenly there are a lot more people talking and not just outside my window
Suddenly the people talking have gotten louder as if only speaking at high volume
    weren't silence

*

Taking off my shoes, I think of people who take their shoes off on airplanes
Taking medicine, I think of people who dream of eternal life

*

Swear at someone, to be righteous; sometimes it's just to let off steam
For a better tomorrow, some people suggest banning all swearing. How's that
    supposed to work?

*

Turn on the computer and the amount of information online swarms like locusts
The disorganization of the internet has assembled into history. So who is
    responsible for forgetting?

*

And history, only when hyperbolized can it be seen
While life which cannot be seen continues through repetition

*

Only life in excess is life other than this there is no life. Some disagree
Only beauty in excess is beauty other than that there is no beauty. Some disagree

*

Excessive stupidity is observed, praised, inquired about
In the end it makes its way out by becoming a joke. Anyone who disagrees is
    just laughing along

*

雪球终于滚不动了只好去滚另一个雪球
猪终于肥不动了终于和人类摊牌要求减肥

*

落日：一个耸听的危言。肃穆的群山变冷。
抒情者呕吐后继续抒情，但自知体力渐渐不行。

2016

*

The snowball ultimately can't roll anymore so go roll another one
Pigs eventually can't get any fatter and eventually confront humanity about
    losing weight

*

Sunset: sensationalist overstatement. The solemn mountains grow cold.
Lyricists still wax lyrical after they vomit but they know their strength is waning.

2016

何谓

何谓扫兴——
好比舞会的大门打开，盛装的女子摔倒。

何谓挫败——
好比就要高潮，忽然地震了或者着火了。

何谓不平——
好比阳光统统卸在了我身旁人的身上。

何谓悲催——
好比毒太阳下两个女人吵架却同时中暑。

何谓不可能——
好比刽子手举刀打喷嚏，受刑者也打喷嚏。

何谓运气——
好比醉汉躺倒在马路上，没有车子开来。

何谓不严肃——
好比驴长出翅膀，不为飞翔只为炫耀。

2016.8.31 / 2018.7.17

What We Call

What we call dispiriting—
Like when ballroom doors open, and a woman in an elegant evening gown slips
    and falls.

What we call defeat—
Like right at the moment of orgasm there's an earthquake or a fire breaks out.

What we call unfairness—
Like when the sun unloads itself on the person right next to me.

What we call pathetic—
Like when two women are fighting under the scorching sun and catch heatstroke.

What we call impossibility—
Like an executioner raising his axe and sneezing, and the condemned sneezes at
    the same time.

What we call luck—
Like a drunk lying in the middle of the street, no cars driving by.

What we call unserious—
Like a donkey with wings, not for flying but just for show.

August 31, 2016 / July 17, 2018

潘家园旧货市场玄思录

美丽的**假**古董是美丽的吗？美丽的**假人**倒可以是美丽的但那是假人。
假人荒着**灵魂**。即使假人人山人海也聚不来山海一般的灵魂！
那么**美丽**是可以自灵魂抽身的吗？

那么垃圾般的**真**古董果真是**垃圾**吗？
认出那垃圾**价值**的人一口咬定那就是垃圾嗯那就是垃圾：
他貌似不在乎才有可能付出一个**垃圾价**。

以垃圾价买一把战国削刀能气死战国刮削竹木简的青铜人。
以今日**存在感**回望战国青铜人，他们全都老实巴交陌生于**全球化的大世面**。
他们怎么就成了**伟人**呢？不解。

战国终了在公元前221年。
青铜物件晚于晋灭吴的280年就已没啥意思。

2000多年前的真古董比200年前的真古董**更是**真古董吗？
20年前假造的古董到今日还是**造假**吗？
"日方中方睨"，惠子说。
你在嘈杂的**市场**提问一串**玄学**问题不觉得**可耻**吗？

你敢说惠子也是可耻的人吗？
他沉浸于玄学提问不仅在嘈杂的**市场**上，
也在他为相十五年的魏国**宫廷**中，也在他二十场败仗之后的**旷野**中。

那么3000年前的真古董是否由于**太真**而显得**不真**呢？
那么4000年前的禹王也不真吗？
顾颉刚**疑古**是对的吗？
即使尧舜禹**三代圣王**是真的也不能证明**地摊**上码放的垃圾货来自彼时。

Abstruse Thoughts at the Panjiayuan Antiques Market

Is a *beautiful fake* antique beautiful? Beautiful *fake people* can be beautiful but
    they're fake.
Fake people are devoid of *souls*. A sea of fake people wouldn't yield a lake of souls!
Then can *beauty* be divorced from soul?

Are junk-like *real* antiques really *junk*?
Someone who recognizes the *value* of junk insists that's junk yeah that's junk:
he has to look like he doesn't care to get a *junk rate*.

To buy a Warring States-era paring knife at a junk rate would piss off the bronze
    men who pared bamboo slats in the Warring States era.
Looking back on the Warring States bronze men with today's *sense of existence*,
    they all seem so overcautiously foreign to *globalized reality*.
How did they become *greats*? I don't get it.

The Warring States ended in 221 BCE.
No bronze items from later than the Jin conquest of Eastern Wu in 280 CE
    mean anything.

Are two-thousand-year-old real antiques *even more* real than two-hundred-
    year-old antiques?
Are counterfeit antiques from twenty years ago still *counterfeit* today?
"The sun in the meridian may be the sun in decline," said Huizi.
Don't you feel *ashamed* asking all these *metaphysical* questions in the din of a
    market?

Would you dare call Huizi shameful?
He was steeped in metaphysical questions not only in the din of the *market*,
but in the *palace* of Wei where he served as minister for fifteen years, and in the
    wilderness after his twenty military defeats.

So do three-thousand-year-old real antiques look *fake* because they're *too real*?
Was King Yu from four thousand years ago unreal, too?
Was the scholar Gu Jiegang right to *doubt antiquity*?
Even if the *three sage kings* Yao, Shun, and Yu were real that still wouldn't prove
    that the junk arranged on the *tarp* truly came from that time.

潘家园上空的每朵云彩都该与彼时的云彩略有**相似**。

······ ······ ······ ······

啊造假者得有多高的**学问**方能造假？
盗墓贼得有多大的胆子才敢与古人**鼻子碰鼻子**在地下借着火把或手电光？

但你以为我不辨东西的**真假**吗？
你以为我的**智力**有问题吗？即使我的智力有问题我的**道德感**也没有问题。

骗子与**道德模范**脸盘相似，他们合称"**人类**"。
而区分骗子与道德模范恐非**易事**。

骗子无意做此区分，道德模范无暇做此区分；
像热锅上的蚂蚁非做区分不可的 乃是既**非**骗子亦非道德模范的人：

亦即介乎骗子与道德模范之间的**人**，
亦即推动**世界**运转的半神、关心下一代健康成长的半人，
亦即80年代初既已闲逛土堆上的**潘家园鬼市**且一直闹嚷至今天的**半鬼**。

而他们是**真人**还是**假人**呢？

假人也有要求**影子**跟随的**权利**亦即申请**身份证**的权利。
而多少身份证**持有者**其实是假人。

Every cloud in the sky above Panjiayuan bears some *similarity* with clouds from
    that time.

....

Oh how *cultivated* must the counterfeiter be to make such counterfeits?
How much *gall* must a *grave robber* have to go *nose to nose* underground with
    the ancients by torchlight or flashlight?

But do you think I can't tell *real* from *fake*?
Do you think there's something wrong with my *intellect*? Even if something
    were wrong with my intellect there'd be nothing wrong with my *morality*.

Liars and *moral exemplars* have similar faces, and add up to "*human being.*"
And distinguishing between liars and moral exemplars is not an *easy* feat.

Liars have no intention to make such distinctions, moral exemplars no time;
like ants on a hot wok these distinctions must be made   neither liars nor
    moral exemplars:

namely *persons* between liars and moral exemplars,
namely *demigods* making *the earth* revolve, and *demihumans* concerned about
    the healthy development of *the next generation*,
namely *demighosts* who sauntered over the dirt heap that was the *Panjiayuan
    ghost market* in the early eighties and have been hooting and howling until
    today.

So are they *real* or are they *fake*?

Even fake people enjoy the *right* to demand being followed by *shadows* namely
    the right to apply for *identification cards*.
So many *holders* of identification cards are actually fakes.

更困难的问题附体于嘈杂的市场：
那**亦真亦假**或**半真半假**之人是否可以要求亦假亦真或半假半真之人的权利？
这不是饶舌或玄思，
因为半真半假的物件无情毁坏了济慈或席勒的"**真、善、美**"。

那理解**亦真亦假**的曹雪芹啊玄思的曹雪芹，
也不懂**半真半假**的物质、道德和政治的世界。
他从未**触碰**过半真半假的**物件**吗？至少他从未到过潘家园。

半真半假的人追求半真半假的**幸福**，
谈半真半假的**恋爱**，对着半真半假的古董发呆；对**正义**的要求也是半真半假。
他们在半真半假的世界上**玩出**亦真亦假的感觉可谓**境界**！

……　……　……　……

星期六或星期天，他们来到潘家园，遛弯，淘宝，梦想**捡漏**；
遇到假人、真人，遇到鬼魂、神明，
遇到半真半假的自己，吓一跳，又**假装**没看见。

潘家园旧货市场位于北京东三环南路潘家园桥西南，占地4.85万平方米。主营古旧物品、珠宝玉石、工艺品、收藏品、装饰品，年成交额达数十亿元。市场拥有4000余家经营商户，经商人员近万人，其中60%的经营者来自北京以外的28个省、市、自治区，涉及汉、回、满、苗、侗、维、藏、蒙、朝鲜等十几个民族。

——百度百科

44

A more difficult question applicable to the din of the market:
Can an *unreal real* person or a person *half real half fake* enjoy the right to be real
    unreal or half fake half real?
This isn't rapping or being abstruse,
since the "*Beauty, Truth, and Goodness*" of Keats or Schiller were unsentimentally
    destroyed by items half real half fake.

Cao Xueqin who knew *the unreal real* oh Cao Xueqin the abstruse,
he knew not the *half real half fake* material, moral, and political world.
Did he never *touch* half real half fake *items*? At any rate he never set foot in
    Panjiayuan.

People half real half fake pursue a *happiness* half real half fake,
fall in *love* half real half fake, and fall into a daze looking at half real half fake
    antiques; their demands for *justice* are also half real half fake.
On a world half real half fake they *gain* a sense of unreal reality we might call
    transcendent!

....

Saturdays or Sundays they come to Panjiayuan, stroll around, treasure hunt, dream
    of *filling in gaps*;
they meet fake people and real people, they meet ghosts and deities,
they are startled running into their half real half fake selves, and *pretend* not to
    have seen them.

Panjiayuan Flea Market is located at the southwest of Panjiayuan bridge, South road
of East third ring road, Chaoyang District, Beijing. Covering an area of 48,500 m²,
it is divided into six sections: Roadside Stands, Ancient Architecture, Classical
Furniture, Modern Collection, Sculpture and Stone Engraving, and the Catering
Section. Trading mostly in antiques, handicrafts, ornaments, and other collectibles,
Panjiayuan has an annual revenue of several hundred million yuan. Having more
than four thousand shop owners, this market has nearly ten thousand shop assistants
in which sixty percent are from the other twenty-eight provinces and municipalities
except Beijing. People here come from a variety of backgrounds, there are more than
ten minorities of Hui, Man, Miao, Dong, Uigur, Mongolian, Korean, and other
ethnic groups of China.

                                                      —*Wikipedia*

潘家园，1200个时代堆起来的垃圾山。
1200万个**梦想家**将这垃圾山摊开在**三代圣王**的天空下。

来了官员又像老板，来了教授又像鲜有进步的老学生，
来了**游手好闲**之徒与**执法犯法**的警察称兄道弟，
来了网上开店的人，以及不开店的貔貅它们真假货**通吃**而**不拉屎**。

只买假古董的人你不知他们是真**笨蛋**还是**另有用意**……

潘家园令**三代圣王**的天空**晕眩**。

唉**鱼龙混杂**之地何者为鱼何者为龙？
鱼乐得变龙，**龙**乐得变鱼吗？
倒推的**理性**说：凡不考虑变鱼的那一定是龙了。是龙便张牙舞爪或睡眼惺忪。

睡眼惺忪的**人**也来了。
他见识过一个**真真假假**的世界，疲倦了，退出了树大招风、树倒猢狲散的**江湖**。

当他重新**露面潘家园**，身上**快乐**的小虫子即时复活。
他见到老相识，到公共厕所撒一泡旧尿，
遇到坑骗过的人，坦然，
遇到收地摊费的管理员说：**嘿嘿，我已洗手不干。**

…… …… …… ……

Panjiayuan, a trash heap of 1200 eras piled on top of each other.
Twelve million *dreamers* spread out this heap beneath the sky of the *three sage kings*.

Here comes an official looking like a boss, here comes a professor looking like
an old student hardly making progress,
here comes an *idler* and a *law-breaking officer of the law* calling each other brother,
here comes an online salesman, and legendary pixiu not for sale online *eating*
real and fake goods but *not shitting them out*.

You never be sure if those who only buy fake antiques are truly *idiots* or if they
have something else in mind . . .

Panjiayuan gives the *three sage kings'* sky *vertigo*.

Oh land of intermingling *fish and dragons* who's the fish and who the dragon?
If *fish* are happy metamorphosing into dragons, are *dragons* happy metamorphosing
into fish?
Reverse *inference* says: what does not consider metamorphosing into a fish must
be a dragon. What is a dragon will bare its fangs and brandish its claws, or
else have eyes heavy with sleep.

Here comes *someone* with eyes heavy with sleep.
Experienced in the *truth and falsehood* of the world, he is weary, and has
extracted himself from the *woods* in which the tall trees attract the gale,
and where the monkeys scatter once the trees fall.

When he *makes an appearance* in Panjiayuan once again, the *happy* lice on his
body are reborn.
He sees his old acquaintances, takes an old piss in the public toilet,
meets people he'd cheated, nonchalantly,
and says to the administrators collecting mat fees: *heh heh*, I've washed my
hands of this.

....

交易之地。这商鞅反对的交易之地，也是**毛主席**反对的交易之地。
以**往昔**，以毛主席做交易这是潘家园。
以假往昔做交易，这是毛主席身后**混合经济**时代的潘家园。

假古董也是**劳动**成果，成本免不了，但以假古董售人那是**不道德**的。
而真古董多为**盗墓**所得，但那也是不道德的。
整个潘家园就是一个不道德的地方。它为何**迷人**？

近朱者赤，在市场保安**乡巴佬**懒洋洋地变成文物专家之后
那**斯文**的老专家就只好**斯文扫地**被蒙骗。
对不起，潘家园也是一个**骗人**的地方。

潘家园也是虚张声势的**法律**睁只眼闭只眼的地方。
对不道德的假古董法律点头放行。
假古董虽令购买者郁闷，但那毕竟不取**人命**也没让**国家**吃亏。

这也是长**知识**的地方，长**对**的知识和**不对**的知识。

这也是**有钱人**偶尔光顾的地方。
所有**摊贩**心照不宣地等待那不露声色的有钱人。
最好是**傻傻的**有钱人。戈多也是个傻瓜。

这也是被**管理**的地方。广播喇叭里管理员例行公事奉劝顾客别上当。
但哪有进潘家园不**上当**的？
听摊贩们习惯性的**赌咒发誓**此起彼伏在潘家园你感觉你活在**珍贵的人间**。

这也是城市与乡村、乡村与外国、现在与古代、现在与现在**结合**的地方。
所以它**不是**现在，不是古代，不是外国，不是乡村，也不是城市。

A *trading* place. This trading place opposed by Shang Yang is also opposed by
   Chairman Mao.
A place where *the past* and *Chairman Mao* are traded is Panjiayuan.
Where a fake past is traded, this is the Panjiayuan of the post-Mao *mixed economy.*

Fake antiques are also the fruits of *labor*, whose cost can never be eradicated,
   but to pass fake antiques on to people is *immoral.*
Most real antiques come about through *grave robbing*, but that's immoral, too.
The entire Panjiayuan is an immoral place. Why is it so *enchanting*?

Play with fire and you're bound to get burned, when the *hick* market security
   guard transforms listlessly into a connoisseur of cultural relics
the *effete* old connoisseur should just *effetely sweep up* and be lied to.
Sorry, Panjiayuan is a place of *lies.*

Panjiayuan is a place of the *law* of sound and fury and one eye open one eye shut.
Where the law lets immoral fake antiques pass with a nod.
Though fake antiques upset the buyer, it's not like anyone *dies* from it or
   national interest suffers.

This is a place for the acquisition of *knowledge, correct* knowledge and *incorrect*
   knowledge.

This is a place *wealthy people* might happen to patronize.
All *peddlers* know intuitively to wait for someone inconspicuously wealthy.
Best are the *stupidly* wealthy. Godot was stupid, too.

This is an *administrated* place. The routine business of administrative voices in
   loudspeakers warning visitors not to get taken in.
But when is anyone at Panjiayuan not *taken in*?
Hearing the peddlers' habitual *swears and vows* undulate across Panjiayuan you
   feel like you're living *amongst valuable people.*

This is a place where city and country, home and abroad, modernity and
   antiquity, the present and the present all *come together.*
So it *isn't* the present, it isn't antiquity, it isn't abroad, it isn't the country, it isn't
   the city.

....

活在**珍贵的人**间你就得相信：**正派人**永远是多数！

小贩们来了，盗墓销赃者、骗子和小偷也来了；三轮车卸下**无用**的东西：

99.9%的假古董与0.1%的真垃圾比赛谁更能卖出**好价钱**。
只有潘家园的价钱是**心灵**的价钱或**心情**的价钱。

从红河石斧到文革袖标，6000年比邻而居。
6000年**能够**比邻而居乃是由于对6000年的**想象**能够比邻而居，
社会主义市场经济的大工地吞吐6000年简直小菜一碟。

五湖四海的人为了售假销赃来到潘家园。
五湖四海造假的乡亲们、盗墓的乡亲们**笑嘻嘻地致富**，
然后在无墓可盗之后过有**道德**的生活同时**售假**。

遮阳伞下摊贩们聊到别人挣的钱时笑嘻嘻，**好像**那是自己的钱，
说到别人娶的媳妇时笑嘻嘻，好像那是自己娶的媳妇。

其实每一个人都**梦想着"诗意的栖居"**。

"诗意的栖居"需借助感悟**人生**的**陈词滥调**，
正是符合道德的陈词滥调。
然而符合道德的陈词滥调有可能是**害人**的。

....

Living *amongst valuable people* you have to believe: the *honest* are always the
  majority!

The peddlers are here, liars, thieves, and traffickers in goods robbed from graves
  are all here; the useless wares unloaded from flatbed tricycles:

The 99.9% fake antiques and the 0.1% real junk compete to see who'll sell for a
  good price.
Only the Panjiayuan price is a price of *the soul* or a price of *impulse.*

From porphyry axes to Cultural Revolution armbands, six thousand years
  become neighbors.
Six thousand years *can* become neighbors because the *imaginings* of six thousand
  years can become neighbors,
The construction site of *the socialist market economy* consumes six thousand years
  like a plate of appetizers.

From the five lakes and four seas people come to Panjiayuan to sell fakes and
  traffic in stolen goods.
Five lakes and four seas of fellow villagers and fellow grave robbers *laugh all the
  way* to *the bank.*
Then when there are no graves left to rob they lead *moral* lives as they *sell fakes.*

Peddlers under awnings laugh about each others' earnings, *like* it was their own
  earnings,
laugh about each others' wives, like it was their own wives.

In fact each one *dreams* of *"dwelling poetically upon this earth."*

"Dwelling poetically upon this earth" relies upon the *cliché* of living *life* to the
  fullest,
which befits the cliché of morality.
And befitting the cliché of morality is most likely *harmful.*

你看，售假者只收**真钱**为了"诗意的栖居"。
假钱有可能数在真货贩子之手，因为**玩假钱的**也在**追求**"诗意的栖居"。
他们从未听说过海德格尔就像海德格尔从未听说过潘家园。

玩假钱的若真想买到假古董那他一定是个真**圣人**。

……　……　……　……

来自三门峡的老苏几乎是个圣人：垃圾价卖垃圾货赢得好名声。
他挣钱有限必然愤愤不平更无暇**幽默**；
他已是100次宣布他要卖假了，并非因卖假更道德些。

别人卖假过**滋润的日子**促使他一步步挪到道德的边缘。

"这啥世道啊！假的就是美的就是好的就一定是招人爱的**你妈个屄！**"

他已是101次宣布他要卖假了。
站在道德的边缘他没看见银盆大脸的**神明**就站在身边。

他时常消失，不知他消失时是否越过了道德的**边界**。
消失时他也许是个假人，
神明再把他捉住**变**回真人**扭送**回潘家园。

不停地说话，老苏累了，停三秒，待天地、岁月**涌现**，他继续说：
"这唐代铜簪子一百块钱你要不要？
我媳妇**民办教师**挣两百块钱一个月你小子还**嫌贵**？"

You see, sellers of fakes only accept *real money* for "dwelling poetically upon
    this earth."
Fake bills may pass through the hands of peddlers of real merchandise, since
    counterfeiters also *pursue* their own "dwelling poetically upon this earth."
They've never heard of Heidegger just like Heidegger never heard of Panjiayuan.

If a counterfeiter really wanted to buy fake antiques he'd be a real *sage*.

…… …… …… ……

Old Su from Sanmenxia is almost a sage: selling junk at a junk rate has won
    him a good reputation.
Indignant at his limited earnings he has no time for *humor*;
He's proclaimed a hundred times that he is going to sell fakes, and that selling
    fakes would make him more moral.

Others' *plush life* from selling fakes pushes him toward the margins of morality.

"What world is this! The fake is beautiful which is good which attracts customers
    which *fuck that fucking shit!*"

He's proclaimed a hundred and one times that he is going to sell fakes.
At the margins of morality he hasn't noticed the *deity* with a large face like a
    silver platter standing beside him.

He often disappears, maybe having crossed the *border* of morality.
Maybe when he disappears he's a fake person,
and the deity seizes him and *transforms* him back into real life *delivering* him
    back to Panjiayuan.

Always talking, Old Su is tired, stops for three seconds, and when heaven and
    earth and time and tide *emerge*, he continues:
"This bronze hairpin from the Tang dynasty is a hundred kuai do you want it?
My wife's a *private school teacher* she brings in two hundred a month and you
    think that's *expensive?*"

老苏眼红而聒噪好像沉默会使他飞离这世界。
在他看来世界即人群，而不在人群之中那是可怕的。
不得已一个人走路，一个人喝酒，一个人唱歌那是可怕的。

要不停地说话。
鸟儿们也在不停地说话所以并不高飞；有谁听到过鸟儿在高天喋喋不休？
风也在说话，不过有时停下。

…… …… …… ……

无法熄灭的往古。
"油炸鬼"作假。或将老玉件煮于沸水30分钟使之还阳。
仿佛阴间是可以自由往来的地方。

唐代不远，汉代也不远，战国人全都站了起来。
看见了孟子和荀子，看见了刘安、刘向、刘歆和刘义庆。
"刘向传经心事违"。
刘歆助王莽篡改《左传》影响至今。

潘家园人见多识广，包括对鬼魂的见识，但说鬼者寥寥，
害怕一旦说出便说出了自己。

鬼魂不做假，但也可以自称是假的吗？
鬼魂是假的那人民币是假的吗？

卖珠子的女人说我真遇到过鬼啊。那鬼，高个子，来到我家门口，头比门框
还高呐，进不来或者不愿进。是他想吓唬我或者给我提个醒。我去庙里烧了
七七四十九天香。把他的东西还给天地。他不再来了。

Red-eyed Old Su shouts as if *silence* would send him flying from the earth.
The way he sees it the world is *people*, and not being among people scares him.
Having no choice but to walk *alone*, to drink alone, to sing alone *scares* him.

Best to keep talking.
Birds are always talking so they don't fly high; who's ever heard of birds
	chirping on while flying high?
The wind talks, too, but *stops* sometimes.

....

The inextinguishable past.
"Frying ghosts" is a kind of fakery. Boiling jade in water for thirty minutes to
	revive it.
As if *the underworld* were a place where you could come and go *as you pleased*.

The Tang is not far, nor the Han, all the people of the Warring States *have stood up*.
I've seen Mencius and Xunzi, I've seen Liu An and Liu Xiang and Liu Xin and
	Liu Yiqing.
"Liu Xiang passed down the classics but my heart's mission failed."
Liu Xin distorted the *Zuozhuan* for the fake emperor Wang Mang with
	repercussions that continue to this day.

The people of Panjiayuan are knowledgeable, even about ghosts, though few
	bring up *ghosts* anymore,
they're afraid their *selves* will slip out if they say too much.

Ghosts don't make fakes, but can they call themselves fake?
If ghosts are fake then can RMB be fake?

The woman selling beads says I've seen a real ghost. It was tall, it came right up
to my door, and its head was higher than the doorway, so it either couldn't
come in or didn't want to. It just wanted to scare me or else give me some kind
of warning. I went to the *temple* and lit incense for seven times seven forty-nine
days. My way to return his things *to heaven*. He never came back.

干宝《搜神记》卷二十载阮瞻素执无鬼论，有客造访聊谈名理，甚有辩才。及鬼神之事，客屈于阮瞻，乃作色曰："即仆便是鬼！"须臾消灭。阮瞻默然，意色大恶。岁余病死。

但潘家园也是**蔑视**死亡的地方，
也是**无神论者**没啥高深题目却高谈阔论的地方，
也是**有神论者**祈求**神明**原谅的地方。

佛、菩萨、基督、天使、土地爷、财神爷、关公、文曲星漫步在潘家园。
他们的木像石像铜像或坐或立在遮阳伞下**不吭一声**。

他们听到陕西小贩说"我不挣小钱"所以要价350万售卖盗墓所得的西周簋。
他们听见天津小贩赌咒发誓："这当然是老玛瑙不是玻璃哒；要玻璃哒我**吃啦**！"

……　……　……　……

倒腾假货的人把自己倒腾成假人，
倒腾死人物件的人倒腾到自己的**死**。

死前他要求用**真药**这是人之常情，死前他面对**万事空**这是普通智力可以达到的。

他最后眺望一眼**星空**在他进入那星空之前，
好像，据说，置身于星空的人只能回望**地球**，看不到其它星星。

他的**恐惧**是千真万确的。眺望星空他的**崇高感**也是千真万确的。
崇高感总是来得**太晚**直到**勾销**真假的**未来**忽然露面。

Fascicle twenty of Gan Bao's *Search for the Supernatural* details Ruan Zhan's insistence in the nonexistence of ghosts, even when a particularly eloquent visitor came to discuss Daoism. When the topic turned to gods and ghosts, the visitor capitulated to Ruan Zhan, though he added: "But I am a ghost!" and vanished. Discountenanced, Ruan Zhan was silent for a long time. Little over a year later he fell ill and died.

But Panjiayuan is a place that *casts a cold eye* on death,
a place where *atheists* declaim but without lofty topics to declaim on,
a place *believers* pray for *the gods* to forgive.

Buddhas, bodhisattvas, Christs, angels, gods of the earth, gods of wealth, Guan Yu,
    and *the constellation Wen Chang* stroll through Panjiayuan.
Their wood and stone figurines and bronze figurines stand or sit under the
    awnings *without making a sound*.

They listen as peddlers from Shaanxi say "I'm not looking for chump change"
    and charge 3,500,000 RMB for a Western Zhou xu cauldron robbed
    from a grave.
They hear a peddler from Tianjin swear: "Of course this is agate and not glass;
    if it's glass I'll *eat* it!"

......　......　......　......

Trafficking in fakes he trafficked himself fake.
Trafficking in goods of the dead he trafficked till he *died*.

Before death he demanded *real medicine* which is just common sense, before
    dying he stared into *the abyss* which basic intellect can achieve.

A last look at the *starry night* before entering that starry night,
the way, as they say, you can only look back at the *earth* from space and cannot
    see the other stars.

His *fear* was real and true. Looking into the starry night his *sense of the sublime*
    was real and true.
The sublime always arrives *too late* until a *future* in which truth and falsity are
    abolished suddenly appears.

在古代，死者惧怕盗墓贼：尤其奉天承运的帝王惧怕盗墓贼。
而今盗墓贼惧怕公安局，公安局惧怕**国家主席**。
国家主席在别的国家就是总统，
在古代就是**皇帝**。

当主席和当总统和当皇帝是一样的**感觉**吗？
你去问袁世凯或者拿破仑。

过去未来你去问**算命先生**，福祸寿夭你去问**和尚、道士**，
升官发财你去问**气功大师**，爱情涨落你去问**知心姐姐**，

对挣钱的**执着**不妨碍对**佛**的执着，而佛，无所执着。
你就别问了！你且住嘴。

…… …… …… ……

潘家园的风吹着潘家园的古今众身影。
《史记.伯夷列传》即使被茶叶水熏黄那也是天地间的**大文章**。

潘家园的司马迁不怕茶叶水。

但司马迁的**寂寞**就是五伯、七雄的寂寞：
就是古战场和帝王陵墓的寂寞、当今**乌烟瘴气**的市场的寂寞。

曾经，寂寞的清东陵来了孙殿英的**土匪兵**。
炸药包炸开地官后土匪兵扣出了慈禧太后嘴里的夜明珠。
然后群山**依旧**寂寞、旷野依旧寂寞。百虫争鸣，**军阀**混战在**中国**的大地上。

In the past, the dead feared grave robbers: especially rulers *ordained by heaven*
    feared grave robbers.
Today grave robbers fear the Public Security Bureau, while the Public Security
    Bureau fears the *Chairman of the People's Republic.*
In other countries the Chairman of the People's Republic is just a president,
but in the past he was *emperor.*

Does it *feel* the same to be chairman and president and emperor?
Go ask Yuan Shikai or maybe Napoleon.

For the past and future go ask a *fortune teller*, for fortune and calamity, longevity
    and death, go ask a *monk or priest,*
for career advancement and getting rich go ask a *qigong master*, for the fluctuations
    of love go ask *your big sister,*

attachment to money does not impede attachment to *the Buddha*, but with the
    Buddha there's nothing to be attached to.
So quit asking—just shut up already!

…… …… …… ……

The wind of Panjiayuan blows past all Panjiayuan's ancient and modern shadows.
Even if the Ranked Biography of Bo Yi from *The Records of the Grand Historian*
    were yellowed from spilled tea it would still be a *literary masterpiece.*

The Sima Qian of Panjiayuan doesn't fear spilled tea.

But the *solitude* of the grand historian is the solitude of five overlords and seven
    powers:
the solitude of ancient battlefields and rulers' mausoleums, the solitude of present-
    day markets with *foul air.*

One time, Sun Dianying's *gang of bandits* came to the solitude of the Eastern
    Qing tombs.
After their satchel charges blew open the underground palace the bandits plucked
    the night-glowing pearl from the Empress Dowager's lips.
Then the mountains *went back* to their solitude, and the wilderness too. As a
    hundred insects chirped, combat entangled the *warlords* across *China.*

而在1800年前。曹操的大军不允许马踩庄稼；
他招能纳士不问德行，对古墓也绝不放过。
他向**死人**要军饷拿下半个中国，但也只拿下半个中国。嘿嘿。

得罪了太多的死人他死前下令薄葬。
1800年后其墓葬被发掘时墓室里值钱的只有玛瑙珠一**颗**。
墓在河南安阳西高穴。真墓？假墓？还是他人之墓？

河南省政府给它挂牌保护以便**开**发**旅游**。
收音机里的《三国演义》**评书**至今没有停播过，即使说评书的业已作古。

真与假，寂寞的**物件**。
半真半假的物件同样享受寂寞的**风雨**、**日光**和**星光**。

而偶见人骨和兽骨的**旷野**，还有大音希声的**群山**　乃是**寂寞本身**。

2014.1.27–2.4
春节的鞭炮声

But 1800 years ago. Cao Cao's army did not permit their horses to trample the crops;
He looked for bare ability over moral conduct, not sparing ancient tombs.
He took over half of China demanding soldiers' provisions from *the dead*, but then
    again he only took over half of China. Heh heh.

Having *insulted* too many of the dead he commanded that his own funeral be frugal.
When his grave was dug up 1800 years later all that was left was *one* agate bead.
His grave is Xigaoxue Tomb No. 2 in Anyang, Henan. A real tomb? A fake tomb?
    Someone else's tomb?

The provincial government of Henan hung a plaque on it for protection and
    the *development of tourism*.
The *Romance of Three Kingdoms* radio *play* is still broadcast, though the narrator
    has already passed.

Real and fake, solitary *items*.
Half real half fake items nevertheless enjoy solitary *wind and rain*, as well as
    sunlight and *starlight*.

While the *wilderness* of occasional human and animal bones, and the *mountains*
    of booming silence   become *solitude itself*.

                January 27–February 4, 2014
                to the firecrackers of Spring Festival

八段诗

1. 哪一朵色情的桃花

哪一朵色情的桃花曾梦见过这只多汁的桃子现在被我咬下一口
并想到这个问题在西王母的蟠桃园中？
我，齐天大圣，偷偷地进来，还得偷偷地出去。

2. 面向大海

面向大海，背向城市。
意图面向海底的城市，珊瑚和水母的城市，5万年前的城市，
却看见了空中的城市，那里游荡着狗熊和山猫，是没有时间的城市。

3. 习惯性想象

一想到蛇，必是毒蛇，仿佛除了毒蛇没有蛇；
一想到鲨鱼，必是吃人的鲨鱼，仿佛全世界都是迪斯尼。
对那些无害的蛇和鲨鱼，作为一个成熟的男人，我要说一声"对不起"。

4. 新江南

天空阴沉这是旧江南。新时代的小鸟飞在旧江南的天空。
旧江南的江面上机动渡轮半新不旧，虽新而旧，走着旧日的斜线。
对岸的楼房盖得比山岭高出一截这已是百分百的新江南。

Eight Fragments

1. *Which Pornographic Peach Blossom*

Which pornographic peach blossom dreamt of me biting into this juicy peach
and thought up this question in the orchard of the Queen of the West?
I, the Monkey King, stole in here—and now I must steal out.

2. *Facing the Sea*

Facing the sea, back toward the city.
Trying to face the city at the bottom of the sea, the city of coral and jellyfish, a
      fifty-thousand-year-old city
but instead seeing the city in the sky, where black bears and leopards roam, a
      city outside of time.

3. *Customary Imaginations*

Think of a snake and it will be a poison snake, as if there were no snakes but
      poison snakes;
think of a shark and it will be a man-eating shark, as if the whole world were Disney.
As a responsible man, I would like to say to all harmless snakes and sharks, *I'm
      sorry.*

4. *A New Jiangnan*

The sky is dreary this is old Jiangnan. Birds of a new era fly through the sky of
      old Jiangnan.
On the river in old Jiangnan the motorized ferry isn't new or old, or is old
      although it's new, describing the arc of an old path.
On the other shore the buildings tower over the mountains this is one hundred
      percent the new Jiangnan.

5. 传统和鬼

有传统的地方人多鬼多，甚至人少鬼多，甚至无人而有鬼。
听一人讲话我知道他是鬼，但我不愿点破：
害怕吓着鬼自己，同时也吓着听他讲话的其他人。

6. 关于原子弹的对话

同事说：我反对原子弹掉下来炸我一个人！
另一位同事说：如果原子弹哑了火，真有可能掉下来砸死你！
再一位同事说：什么境界呀你们这是？要是原子弹袭来你们先撤，我顶着！

7. 老演员

老演员演别人，一辈子活六十辈子，可以了。
终于到了戏演完的时候，酸甜苦辣还在继续。
老演员演别人终于演到了自己的死。请安静一会儿，请关灯。

8. 小演员

化了装的准备登台的小姑娘粉衣粉裤，肩膀露在风里。
她既不快乐也不悲伤，像其他小姑娘一样。
在迈步登上那古老的露天舞台之前的一瞬间　她提了提裤子。

2009 / 2011

64

5. *Tradition and Ghosts*

In traditional places there are as many ghosts as people, or even more ghosts than
        people, or even only ghosts and no people.
I hear someone talking and know that he's a ghost, but I don't want to mention it:
I'm afraid of scaring the ghost, and afraid of scaring the people listening to the ghost.

6. *A Dialogue on an Atom Bomb*

One colleague said: I'm opposed to an atom bomb coming down and blowing
        up only me!
Another colleague said: Even if it were a dud, an atom bomb could still come down
        and crush you!
Yet another colleague said: What are you talking about? When the atom bomb
        comes you two just run off, I'll take care of it!

7. *The Old Actor*

The old actor acts as others, living sixty lives in one life, sure.
Finally reaching the end of the act, all of life's bitterness and sweetness remain.
The old actor acts as others up to his own death. Be quiet please, turn out the
        lights please.

8. *The Little Actress*

In makeup about to step onstage in pink shirt and pink pants, the little girl
        bares her shoulders to the wind.
She is neither happy nor sad, like all other girls.
The instant before walking onto that old open-air platform she hikes up her pants.

2009 / 2011

麻烦

空调需要加氟了，旧了。
需要加氟的空调更加敌视看不见的大气了。
大气中的核放射物质像抢购碘盐的人拉也拦不住了。
愚蠢一旦变成时尚就拦也拦不住了。——哎慌张的人总是可怜的。
黄河流域出现长江流域的气候了。乱了。
伏在北方原本干裂的木桌上可以写杏花春雨的诗篇了。
霍金，那个伦敦的外星人，用金属声预言地球坚持不了200年了。
可我居住的城市还装嫩呢，楼房还在长个呢。祝它们坚持发育1000年。
我原本居住在市中心，搬出来就搬不回去了。市中心全建成酒店了。
临时生活或极昂贵或极便宜。但愿地震也是道德的，别震穷人的房子。
穷人和富人互不需要的小资趣味现在殊途同归了。
西方和东方的浪漫相互需要，也殊途同归了。我要去拉萨那最高的人间呢。
可是现实一点儿吧，请现实一点儿，——我60年代的牙又需要补了。
到了坏牙的年龄我爱上诸子百家这老人的学问和春秋战国的星空了。
我知道死人也不是安静的，但两千多年前的死人好一些。
他们不操心煤气灶两个炉孔坏掉一个这类事。——我叫的维修工还没来呢。
我的水管漏了，虽不严重但地板已经拱起，仿佛在闹鬼。
我的房顶被楼上那个热爱钻探的家伙给钻穿了，他也不道谦。
他越来越大胆地活成一个不会道歉的人了，——鬼都怕他。

Annoyances

The A/C is old and needs Freon.

A/C units that need Freon make enemies with the invisible atmosphere.

The radioactive matter in the atmosphere can't be held back, like shoppers
stockpiling iodized salt.

Once stupidity is in style it can't be held back. —Oh these flustered people are
so pitiful.

The climate of the Yangtze River basin shows up in the Yellow River basin.
What a mess.

Poems about apricot blossoms and spring rain can be written on a cracked
wooden table in the north.

Hawking, that London extraterrestrial, uses the sound of metal to prophesy
that the earth won't make it another two hundred years.

But the city I live in is still acting young, with buildings still growing. May they
continue to develop for a thousand years.

I used to live downtown, but once you move out you can never go back.
Downtown is all hotels now.

Life on the fly is either super expensive or super cheap. If only earthquakes were
moral, and didn't tear down poor people's homes.

The poor and the rich don't need each other's petty bourgeois taste now it's just
different paths to the same destination.

The East and the West need each other's romance: different paths to the same
destination. I want to go to the heights of humanity in Lhasa.

But let's be realistic, please—my teeth from the sixties need a filling.

At the age teeth go bad I fall in love with the old-man philosophy of the
Hundred Schools of Thought and the starry skies of the Warring States.

I know the dead aren't quiet, but they're a little better when they've been gone
two thousand years.

They don't worry when one of their two gas burners breaks. —The repairman I
called hasn't shown up yet.

My pipes are leaking. It's not serious but the floor is warped, like it's possessed.

My ceiling has been drilled through by my upstairs neighbor who likes drilling
for things, and he hasn't even apologized.

He gets bolder and bolder living as someone who doesn't apologize—even
ghosts fear him.

他以为可以装修出一个世界。祝贺他抢占了一个与时俱进的崭新的自我。

我房顶上的灯泡还亮着，——有电。百度比Google更有电。

不明白李耳为什么变成右派了，而左派为什么靠近孔丘了。

感觉左也不是右也不是，你就自我证明是个中国人了。

站在三岔路口上不知何去何从，杨子就哭了，而我撒了泡中国尿，意识到自己是中国人。

不论你抬头看没看见月亮只要你能背诵"床前明月光"你就是中国人了。

你想站在西方的月亮下大声背诵《独立宣言》你就逃不脱做中国人的命运了。

仅中国和西方还搭不成世界我告诉你，还有身毒和大月支。

拜观音，拜太上老君，烧香如放火，你除了是中国人还能是谁呢？

你内佛外道或者外佛内道，四大皆空却依然我执，你除了是中国人还能是谁呢？

拜上帝的洪秀全把自己拜成了耶稣的弟弟，是中国人都明白这是咋回事。

复杂吗？想想。但你从不想何谓中国人你乃是真正的中国人。

中国人对付中国人：里通外国罚款200，乱闯红灯也罚款200，大概是这样。

听江上一声大雁，只有中国人为憋不出诗句而着急，大概是这样。

喝茶与喝咖啡，口味不同而已，但都需好山环列，好水过眼前。

偷税漏税盖豪宅于山水之间，骂当权者于山水之间，不亦快哉！操！

He thought he could build a world with his renovations. Congratulations to
    him for commandeering a brand new self that can keep up with the times.
The lightbulbs in my ceiling are still bright—there's still power. Baidu has more
    power than Google.
I don't get how Laozi became a rightist, and the left started gesturing toward
    Confucius.
If you don't feel either left or right, you've just proven yourself Chinese.
Standing at a fork in the road not knowing where to go, Yangzi cried, but I
    took a Chinese piss, realizing I was Chinese.
It doesn't matter whether you see the moon when you raise your head, if you
    know all the words to "Quiet Night Thoughts" you're Chinese.
You can't cast off the fate of being Chinese even if you stand beneath the
    Western moon and recite the Declaration of Independence at the top of
    your lungs.
But I tell you there's more than just China and the West in the world, there's
    Singhu and Tokhara.
Praying to the bodhisattva Guanyin, praying to the Grand Supreme Elderly
    Lord, burning incense like a bonfire, what could you be but Chinese?
Whether you're internally Buddhist and externally Daoist, or externally
    Buddhist and internally Daoist, the sensuous world is illusory yet your ego
    is still here, what could you be but Chinese?
Hong Xiuquan prayed to God so hard he made himself Jesus's little brother—
    all Chinese people know what that was about.
Confused? Think about it. But you're only really Chinese if you never think
    about what it means to be Chinese.
How Chinese people treat Chinese people, more or less: a 200 RMB fine for
    selling state secrets, and a 200 RMB fine for running a red light, pretty
    much.
Hearing a wild goose cry on the river, only Chinese people, pretty much, will
    worry about not being able to bite back a line of poetry.
Coffee vs. tea is just a difference in taste, but either way you have to be sur-
    rounded by good mountains, with the purest stream water flowing before
    you.
Is it not pleasant to commit tax evasion so as to build a mansion in the
    mountains? Is it not delightful to curse the authorities in the mountains?
    Fuck off!

摸着石头过河可河水太深了。——智者乐水。

河上的船漏了，船上的修补派和凿沉派两拨人打起来了。

凿沉派骂修补派不是好鹦鹉因为他们学舌还不承认。

修补派回应你们才是鹦鹉因为你们真正在学舌。

河上的船漏了，岸上看热闹的人起哄了，如在唐朝在宋朝。

人一起哄就变得年轻了，不管三七二十一了。

新闻走在事实前头是好作家和坏记者的共同梦想。

而在摄影机前一本正经是阴谋家的常态。

常态，我要说的正是常态，如政治问题总被道德化。

而今道德问题又被男女关系化了。

而男女关系成了贪官们最令人津津乐道的话题了。

谁浪漫也不如贪官们更浪漫。

但不男不女已在青年人中时髦好几年了。

一转眼我儿子就要上初中了。

儿子的数学题我已经不会做了。

我要喝杯冰水，忽然想到

该换个大号冰箱了。

2010.10 / 2017.4

Cross the river by feeling the stones, but the water's too deep. —The wise find
     pleasure in water.
The boat on the river is leaking, and the repairists and the sinkists are fighting.
The sinkists say the repairists aren't good parrots since they don't admit they're
     repeating other people's words.
The repairists respond that the sinkists are the real parrots since they're the ones
     repeating other people's words.
The boat on the river is leaking, and those watching from the shore start
     jeering, like it was the Tang or the Song dynasty.
Once people start jeering they get younger, throwing caution to the wind.
News that comes before reality is the common dream of good authors and bad
     journalists.
But conspirators are usually earnest before the camera.
The *usual* is what I want to talk about, like political issues being made into
     moral issues.
And now moral issues are made into relations between men and women.
And relations between men and women are what people gossip about when it
     comes to corrupt officials.
However romantic you are, you won't be more romantic than a corrupt official.
But androgyny has been in style among young people for years.
In the blink of an eye my son's about to start junior high.
I can't even do his math homework.
I want a glass of ice water and then remember:
I need to get a bigger refrigerator.

October 2010 / April 2017

出行日记

1. 撞死在挡风玻璃上的蝴蝶

我把车子开上高速公路，就是开始了一场对蝴蝶的屠杀；或者蝴蝶看到我高速驶来，就决定发动一场自杀飞行。它们撞死在挡风玻璃上。它们偏偏撞死在我的挡风玻璃上。一只只死去，变成水滴，变成雨刷刮不去的黄色斑迹。我只好停车，一半为了哀悼，一半为了拖延欠债还钱的时刻。但立刻来了警察，查验我的证件，向我开出罚单，命令我立刻上路，不得在高速公路上停车。立刻便有更多的蝴蝶撞死在我的挡风玻璃上。

2. 逆行

忽然就只剩下我一辆车了。忽然就望见天上落下羊群了。忽然迎面而来的羊一只只全变成了车辆。忽然双行道变成了单行道。走着走着，忽然我就逆行了！我怎么开上了这条路？那些与我同路的车辆去了哪里？我逆着所有的车辆，仿佛逆着真善美的羊群。不是我要撞死它们，而是它们要将我温柔地踩死。走着走着，忽然我就逆行了！我就听到了风声，还有大地的安静。我没撞上任何车辆，我撞上了虚无。

3. 我顺便看见了日出

时隔二十年重返北戴河海滨。当年海滩上的姑娘皆已生儿育女。我带来我的儿子，他将第一次见识什么叫大海日出。但他牙疼了一夜，我心疼了一夜——可怜的、幼小的孩子!大海在窗外聚义，我不曾注意；大海涌进房间，又退出房间，没有留下一丝痕迹。我是为日出而来：日出和大海(这是我最后一点浪漫情怀)。但我为孩子的牙疼忙活了一夜。第二天早晨我即将入睡时顺便看见了日出。

Travel Diary

1. *The Butterflies that Die on My Windshield*

To drive my car onto the highway is to begin a slaughter of butterflies; or, the butterflies see me speeding along and decide to undertake a suicide mission. They die on windshields. They die on *my* windshield. One after another they die, turning into droplets of water, turning into yellow streaks the windshield wipers cannot wipe away. I have to pull over—to mourn, but also to put off paying my own debt. Immediately a policeman shows up, inspects my license, issues me a ticket, and orders me to leave, warning me against standing on the shoulder. And immediately more butterflies start dying on my windshield.

2. *The Wrong Way*

Suddenly all that's left is my car. Suddenly I see a flock of sheep falling from the sky. Suddenly the sheep coming toward me turn into cars, one after another. Suddenly the two-lane highway turns into a one-way street. Driving along, suddenly I find I'm going the wrong way! How did I end up on this road? Where did all the other cars disappear to? Driving against traffic is like driving against the sheep of Truth, Goodness, and Beauty. It's not me trying to kill them; it's them about to trample me gently. Driving along, suddenly I find I'm going the wrong way! I hear the sound of wind and the silence of the earth. I don't run into any cars— what I run into is nothingness.

3. *I Happen to See the Sunrise*

After twenty years I return to the Beidaihe seaside. The beach girls of those years all have children of their own now. I've brought my son, so he can see the sunrise over the sea for the first time. But he was up all night with a toothache, and I was up all night with heartache—poor little boy! The sea rises up outside the window, which I'd never noticed; the sea rushes into our room, then retreats, without leaving a single mark. I came for the sunrise: the sunrise and the sea (this is the final sentiment of my Romanticism). But I was running around all night because of my son's toothache. The next morning I happen to see the sunrise right as I'm about to fall asleep.

4. 小镇上的骆一禾

小镇：三条大街、一座广场、五千棵树、一个朋友。朋友请我吃饭，在燕赵豪杰饭庄。朋友带来六个人，其中一人让我吃惊：这是骆一禾吗？但一禾已逝去十五年！此人模样、神态酷似一禾；但个头比一禾高，书读得比一禾少。我们握手；他亲切又腼腆。一禾不知道另有一个骆一禾；一禾去世以后这另一个骆一禾依然默默地活着。此事我从未向人提起，包括一禾的遗孀。我守着这个"秘密"直到今天，说不清为什么。

5. 小镇时尚

为什么这小镇上的女人人人头戴大盖帽？而光头缩脖子的男人们，蹲在街头，端着海碗吃面条。女人们买菜，买鞋垫，街头聊天，人人头戴大盖帽。解放军的大盖帽、工商管理员的大盖帽、警察的大盖帽、邮递员的大盖帽。但在小镇上，所有应该头戴大盖帽的人其实难得一见。戴大盖帽的女人们身穿花毛衣，不严肃也不恶作剧。也许她们觉得美极了大盖帽。或者，她们出门时只是想戴顶帽子，随手一抓，全是大盖帽。

6. 穿过菜市场

黄昏，（古代诗人思维最活跃的时刻。漫步在斜阳浸染的山道上何等快意！）我一边羡慕着古代诗人，一边穿过这满地烂菜叶的菜市场。我身边没有一个人长得像仙鹤，没有一个土豆长得像岩石，没有一根芹菜长得像松树。但这毕竟是我的黄昏：一个满不在乎、穿着睡衣拖鞋，嘴里嗑着瓜籽儿的女人逆光走来。菜市场的斜阳把她身体的轮廓映得一清二楚。她假装不知道她几乎赤裸，我假装没看见以免别人看到我心中忐忑。

4. *Luo Yihe in a Small Town*

Small town: three streets, a square, five thousand trees, one friend. This friend invites me to dinner, at a restaurant called The Heroes of Yan and Zhao. The friend brings six others, one of whom shocked me: could this be Luo Yihe? But Yihe has been dead for over fifteen years! This man's looks and demeanor are exactly like Yihe's; but he's taller than Yihe and hasn't read as much. We shake hands; he's cordial but shy. Yihe never knew there was another Yihe; after Yihe died this other Luo Yihe secretly kept on living. I've never mentioned this to anyone, not even to Yihe's widow. I've kept this "secret" until today, though I can't say why.

5. *Small Town Fashion*

Why do all the women in this town wear peaked caps? And the bald men with shrunken necks squat on the street, eating big bowls of noodles. The women buy groceries and insoles and chat on the street, each wearing a peaked cap. People's Liberation Army peaked caps and civil administration peaked caps and police officer peaked caps and postal service peaked caps. But it's hard to find anyone in this town who actually should be wearing a peaked cap. The peaked-cap women wear floral sweaters, neither serious nor mischievous. Maybe they think these peaked caps are the height of beauty. Or maybe when they go out they just want to wear a hat, and all they happen to grab when they reach for one is a peaked hat.

6. *Walking through the Market*

At dusk (when ancient poets' minds were most active—what joy to meander through mountain paths in the tint of the slanting sun!), I'm envious of the ancient poets as I walk through a market of rotting leafy vegetables. Nobody near me looks like a red-crowned crane, no potatoes look like a cliff, and no celery stalks look like pine trees. But it is my dusk, after all: a backlit woman comes toward me, indifferent, dressed in pajamas and sandals, munching on sunflower seeds. The light of the slanting sun outlines her frame in the market. She pretends not to know she's almost naked, and I pretend not to see her in case anyone can tell the disturbances in my heart.

7. 这座城市避开了我

这座城市避开了我。它给我大雨，使我不能在街头闲逛。我听说过的博物馆，因人手不够而闭馆。商店里，人们说着我听不懂的话。商店里只卖一种酒，是我不能喝的那一种。我饥肠辘辘找到的，是关了门的餐厅。我大声抱怨，但没人在乎。我敲沿街的门，门开了，但屋里却没有人。我靠到一棵树上，树叶便落了下来。在这座城市里我没有一个熟人。哎，我到了这座城市，等于没有到过。

8. 一个发现

你提箱子出门，乘飞机乘火车乘汽车。你抵达你计划要抵达或没计划要抵达的地方，洗把脸或洗个澡，然后走出旅店。你想看一看这陌生的地方——陌生的城市或者陌生的乡村，你会发现，其实你无法走出很远。你跨越千山，只是为了见识千山之外的一条或几条街道、一张或几张面孔、一座或几座山头。你抵达你计划要抵达或没计划要抵达的地方，然后走出旅店。但其实你真地无法走出很远。这话说出来像一个诅咒，但我不是故意的。

9. 另一个发现

我走到哪儿，我头上的月亮就跟到哪儿，但月亮并不了解我的心思。我吃什么，来到我身旁的狗就也吃什么，但我和这条狗并不是同类。蟑螂跟我住在同一间屋子里，我们需要同样的生存温度，但我还是在今天早晨用杀虫剂喷死了七只蟑螂。飞鸟看到了我所看到的社会的不公正，但我们并不因此分享同一种愤怒。即使落叶与我同时感受到秋天的来临，我也不能肯定落叶之间曾经互致爱慕，互致同情。

7. *This City Avoids Me*

This city avoids me. It gives me rainstorms, so I can't walk around outside. The museum I'd heard about has closed due to staffing issues. In the store people say things I can't understand. They only sell one kind of liquor at the store, the kind I can't drink. Stomach rumbling, I find a restaurant, but it's closed. I complain loudly, but no one cares. I knock on the side door in the alley and it opens, but no one's inside. I lean on a tree and the leaves fall. I don't know anyone in this city. Coming to this city, it's like I never got here.

8. *A Discovery*

You pick up your suitcase and go out, taking an airplane taking a train taking a bus. You arrive at the destination where you planned to arrive or where you did not plan to arrive, wash your face or take a shower, and then leave the hotel. You want to look around in this unfamiliar place—this unfamiliar city or unfamiliar village, but as you discover, you can't go very far. You crossed a thousand mountains, only to see on the other side of those mountains a few streets or one street, a few faces or one face, a few hills or one hill. You arrive at the destination where you planned to arrive or where you did not plan to arrive, and then leave the hotel. But you can't go very far. It sounds like a curse, but I don't mean it like that.

9. *Another Discovery*

Wherever I go, the moon overhead follows me, but the moon doesn't know my mind. Whatever I eat the dog comes over to eat, but the dog and I aren't the same. Cockroaches live in the same home as me, and we need the same room temperature to survive in, but just this morning I killed seven of them with insecticide. Birds see the same inequities of society that I see, but this doesn't mean we can share our outrage. Even if falling leaves and I feel the same arrival of autumn, I can't be sure if these leaves ever admired each other, or if they have any sympathy for each other.

10. 变幻

黑夜和小雨使我迷路。在一段停着压路机却无人施工的路面上，一个胖子跟上了我。我加快脚步。他开始威胁和谩骂。我并不焦虑我兜里不多的钱，我焦虑这城市里只有他和我。焦虑，焦急，我一阵虚弱，忽然我就变成了三个人。我们三人停步转身，已经冲到眼前的胖子完全傻眼。他回身就跑，我们拔脚就追。我们边跑边体验人多势众的感觉真好。直到我们一起掉下一道水沟，直到我找不到我那同伴二人。

11. 黑夜里两个吵架的人

我吸烟。烟雾被窗外的黑夜吸走。黑夜寂静，鼓励无眠的人们发出声响。于是我就听见了两人吵架的声音。吵架声来自另一个窗口（我看不见的窗口）。我忽然觉得每一个窗口后面都有人倾听。我听见男人高喊："你给我滚！"我听见女人毫不示弱："这房子是我的！"我听见男人长篇大论地谩骂，我听见女人长篇大论地啼哭。……黑夜。黑夜。黑夜。我学了声鸡叫，天就亮了。吵架的人终于住口。

12. 罪过和罪过

内急使我急不择路，内急释放使我舒畅。哆嗦了一下，我才看见——在没有隔断的公共厕所——怎么回事？——左右两个女孩，也站着撒尿。那场景令我惊讶：那两个女孩竟敢激进反抗她们撒尿的传统。我正想夸她们勇敢，她们迅速摆出良家妇女的做派。她们从隔壁招呼来男人把我扭送派出所。我作为流氓轰轰烈烈地穿过大街。我问警察是我误进女厕所的罪过大，还是女人站着撒尿的罪过大。警察答不上这个智力难题，就把我放了。

10. *Transformation*

I get lost in the night and rain. On a road with a stopped steamroller and no one working construction, a fat guy catches up to me. I speed up. He starts threatening, hurling abuse. I'm not worried about the bit of money in my pocket, I'm worried about there being no one in this city but me and him. Anxious, worried, I get weak, then suddenly turn into three people. We turn around, all three of us, and the fat guy before us is dumbstruck. He turns and runs, and we give chase. We run, experiencing the power and joy of strength in numbers. Until we all fall into a ditch . . . until I can't find the other two of me.

11. *A Couple Arguing in the Night*

I smoke. The smoke is sucked into the night outside the window. The night is silent, inviting noises from the sleepless. So I hear the sounds of two people arguing. The sounds of an argument come from a different window (a window I cannot see). Suddenly I feel that behind every window must be someone listening. I hear a man shout: "Get the hell out of here!" I hear a woman not give an inch: "This house is mine!" I hear the man let loose an abusive diatribe, and the woman an invective of sobs. . . . Night. Night. Night. I cry out like a rooster, and the sky brightens. Finally the arguing couple shuts their mouths.

12. *Crime and Crime*

I'm in such a rush I don't look where I'm going, but then I relieve myself and I'm worry free. I shiver, and then notice—in the unpartitioned public toilet— huh?—two girls left and right of me, standing there pissing, too. The scene stuns me: these girls are so audacious they've revolted against their entire tradition of pissing. I want to praise their bravery, but then they start to act like upstanding ladies from respectable homes. They call outside to have me taken into custody. In a spectacle I'm paraded across the street as a pervert. I ask the officer which crime is worse, entering the women's room by mistake or pissing standing up. The officer can't answer this riddle, so I'm let go.

13. 袜子广告

走过卖袜子的广告牌。广告牌上说"这正是买袜子的好时节"。这为什么不是补袜子的好时节？这为什么不是脱袜子的好时节？所谓小康社会，就是人人可以在穿鞋之前穿上袜子；所谓富足社会，就是有人不屑于在穿鞋之前穿上袜子。我猜走过我身旁的人，有一个的袜子已经被脚趾洞穿；另一个是臭脚，然而袜子完好。我猜我的袜子有点羡慕那些新袜子。我猜我的双脚有点羡慕阳光下的赤脚。

14. 尴尬

巨大的阳台上，一群吃饭的人。我举止得体，谈吐配得上那十八世纪的建筑和大有来历的餐具。但我不该得意忘形，不该急于表达我对这世界的真实看法。报应来了。西瓜呛进我的气管。我控制不住我的咳嗽，不得不离开餐桌。一块呛进我气管的西瓜逼我领受我必得的羞辱，因为我咳嗽得过于真实。他们看着我，同情我的尴尬，然后继续他们关于世界的不真实的谈话。他们甚至比我大声咳嗽开始之前更文雅。

15. 洗澡感想

浴缸是别人用过的。不过没什么——手里的钞票也是别人攥过的，头上的月亮也是别人赞美过的。但依然，这是别人用过的浴缸。是女人用过的还是男人用过的？是漂亮女人用过的还是恶俗男人用过的？不过没什么——在异地还能有个浴缸洗澡就算幸运了。我告诫自己，应该认命地、默默地生活，包括认命地、默默地用别人的浴缸洗自己的澡。不过我一默默，蟑螂就从犄角旮旯里摸了出来。不过没什么——没有老鼠出来就算幸运了。

13. *Sock Advertisement*

I walk past a billboard selling socks. The billboard says, "Now is the time to buy socks!" Why isn't this the time to mend socks? Why isn't this the time to take off socks? A well-off society is a society in which everyone can put on socks before shoes; an affluent society is one in which some don't bother putting on socks before shoes. I bet at least one of these people walking by me has holes in their socks; another must have stinky feet, but socks intact. I bet my own socks are jealous of new socks. I bet my feet are jealous of bare feet soaking in the sun.

14. *Awkward*

On a grand balcony, a group of people eating. My speech and demeanor befit the eighteenth-century architecture and historical cutlery. But I must not get carried away, must not be too eager to express my actual thoughts on the state of the world. Here comes karma. Some watermelon gets stuck in my trachea. I can't keep from coughing, and have to leave the table. The watermelon caught in my trachea forces me to accept my deserved shame, because coughing is too honest. They're looking at me, sympathizing with my awkwardness, but then keep on with their disingenuous discourses about the world. They're even more gracious than they were before I started my coughing fit.

15. *Bathing Thoughts*

Someone has used this bathtub. But no problem—someone has handled the money in my hand, and someone has praised the beauty of the moon overhead. But still, someone has used this bathtub. Was it a woman or man? A pretty woman or a hideous man? But no problem—in some places you'd be lucky just to have a bathtub to bathe in. I admonish myself, You should live with fortitude, with restraint, and so bathe in a used bathtub with fortitude and restraint. But as soon as I'm restrained, the cockroaches are going to come creeping out of their nooks and crannies. But no problem—you should count yourself lucky there aren't any mice.

16. 坐在一家麦当劳里

我注视着门口。进来一个背粉红色双肩包的女孩。进来一个戴耳机和墨镜的男孩。进来一个男人、一个女人，在门外他们是搂着的，进门时才松开手。进来一个面无表情的男人，带进一个小女孩，也面无表情。进来一个边进门边阅读手机短信的笑眯眯的女人。进来一个转了一圈,张望了一下，又出去的半老男人……他们每个人都有一个名字、一张嘴、一个胃、一副生殖器。在数到第十七个进来的人时，我站起来，带着我的一套家伙走出去。

17. 有人

有人在上海活一辈子，有人在罗马活一辈子，有人在沙漠的绿洲里活一辈子，有人在雪山脚下活一辈子——你从未见过他们。有人从上海出发，死在雪山脚下；有人从绿洲出发，几乎死在罗马，却最终回到绿洲——你从未见过他们。我写下这些字句，没读过这些字句的人也活一辈子；读到这些字句的人也许会说，这人说的全是废话。且慢，我见过你吗？我想来想去没见过你。我们各活一辈子，也许在同一座城市，同一个小区。

2004 / 2005 / 2007

16. *Sitting in a McDonald's*

I'm staring at the door. A girl with a pink backpack comes in. A boy with earphones and sunglasses comes in. A man and a woman come in, arms around each other in the doorway, letting each other go once inside. A man with a blank expression comes in, leading a small girl, who also has a blank expression. A woman comes in smiling at the text message she's reading on her phone. An old man comes in, looks around, and leaves . . . .. They all have names, mouths, stomachs, reproductive organs. Counting the seventeen people who've come in, I stand up and leave with all my stuff.

17. *Someone*

Someone in Shanghai is living a life, someone in an oasis in the desert is living a life, someone at the foot of a snow-capped mountain is living a life—you've never met them. Someone leaves Shanghai and dies at the foot of a snow-capped mountain; someone leaves an oasis, almost dies in Rome, then makes it back to the oasis—you've never met them. I write these words, but someone who's never read these words is living a life; maybe someone who reads these words will say, Nothing this guy says makes any sense. But wait, have I met you? I think and think, but we've never met. Each of us is living a life, maybe even in the same city, maybe even the same neighborhood.

2004 / 2005 / 2007

西川省纪行

满街的胡琴啊　满街的唱。
满街的小买卖　大喇喇的天。
满街的闺女　都叫翠兰。
满街的大妈　热情的脸。

满街的好人　这不是天堂。
做坏人到头来　必孤单。
信神的头顶着　白帽子。
不信神的也一溜　端着饭碗。

满城的小鸟　想吃羊肉。
三万只绵羊　往城里赶。
看得毛驴大叔们　出冷汗。
一泡泡驴尿　尿街边。

所以随地小便的　是驴下的，
就像缺心眼儿的　全是马养的。
那坑人害人的　如何比？
定是骡子群里　长大的。

手抓手的男女　是褪了色的。
喝酒骂人　是祖传的。
奥迪A6　是奔汉朝的。
刚出厂的旧三轮　是电动的。

亮花花的太阳光　急刹刹的雨，
沙葱韭菜　可劲地绿。
一根筋的黄河　它不回头。
你小子开心　就扒开嗓子吼。

你小子不开心　也扒开嗓子吼。
当知有命无心　不忧愁。
忽然满城的麻将　全开打。
满街的下一代　玩不够。

2014.8.19

84

Travels in Xichuan Province

Everywhere the *erhu* all about the street   oh the whole street singing.
Everywhere the peddlers all about the street   the great big sky.
Everywhere the daughters all about the street   each one named Jade Orchid.
Everywhere the aunties all about the street   all with eager faces.

Everywhere good people all about the street   but this isn't heaven.
Each and every bad man   always ends up lonely.
On each head of each believer   a little white cap.
The nonbelievers sneak off too   with their bowls in hand.

Everywhere little birds all about the city   hungering for mutton.
Thirty thousand lambs   stampeding the city.
When the donkeys see it   they break out in cold sweat.
Streams of donkey piss   trickling down the street.

So if you pee in public   you descend from donkeys.
Just like if you are insolent   you were raised by horses.
But the deceitful and the harmful   what about them?
I say they must have grown up   in a pack of mules.

Boys and girls hold hands   they're wearing faded colors.
The drinking and the swearing   are ancestral tradition.
Each and every Audi A6   is driving to the Han Dynasty.
Newly produced old tricycles   come with electric motors.

All the dazzling sunlight   all the driving rain,
Mongolian onion and Chinese chives   all a vigorous green.
The pigheaded Yellow River   never looks back.
If you're feeling happy kid   then open your mouth and howl.

If you aren't feeling happy kid   open your mouth and howl.
You won't be depressed kid   living without a heart.
Mahjong games throughout the city   suddenly break out.
The next generation all about the street   can never get enough.

August 19, 2014

对人民的疑问

人民没有面孔，有面孔的是张三李四
甚至连张三李四也面孔模糊
面孔清晰的是贾宝玉和林黛玉
面孔更清晰的是贾宝玉和林黛玉的扮演者

如果你是疯子你就不是人民，
如果你是怪人你就不是人民，
人民感冒发烧但人民既不疯也不怪
人民在窃珠者和窃国者之间划出界限

人民里的领头人不是人民
人民里的领头人有可能被人民打倒
被人民打倒的人有可能被人民平反
人民好任性啊但人民没有面孔

洁身自好就是放弃了面孔在人民之中
甘于平庸就是不讨论面孔这回事
而被判处死刑就是被人民开除并被赋予面孔
而被判处死缓说明人民犹豫是否要开恩

远方的人民是美丽的
远方的人民是沉默的大多数
当人民嗡嗡作响，人民就来到近旁
爱远方和不爱远方的人争吵，人民听着

远方的人民就是人类吧?
当人民来到近旁他们是人民还是人类?
有什么区别吗?可能的区别是
人类只能被爱不能被驱遣但人民不是

2015.7.3

Questions About the People

The People have no face, those with a face are Zhang and Li
Even if Zhang's and Li's faces are indistinct
The distinct faces are Jia Baoyu's and Lin Daiyu's
The more distinct faces are the actors' playing Jia Baoyu and Lin Daiyu

If you are crazy you are not the People
If you are odd you are not the People
The People can catch a cold or run a fever but never be crazy or odd
The People draw a border between those who steal a little and those who steal a lot

The leader of the People is not the People
The leader of the People could be overthrown by the People
Anyone overthrown by the People could be rehabilitated by the People
The People are capricious but the People have no face

To stay out of trouble is to give up your face among the People
To be content with a quiet life is to not discuss the matter of faces
But to be sentenced to death is to be banished by the People but given a face
But to be sentenced to death with reprieve implies the People are unsure about
      being merciful

In the distance the People are beautiful
In the distance the People are a silent majority
When the People are noisy, the People have come near
People who love distance argue with people who don't love distance, and the
      People listen

Are the People in the distance people?
When the People come near are they the People or are they people?
What's the difference? Maybe the difference
Is that people can be loved or deported, but the People cannot

July 3, 2015

蠢话

那蠢话"要成为你自己"我牢记了多年现在才开窍：
你不太可能成为你自己，你有可能成为百千个他人。
没有一只鸟不会飞，没有一只猴子会弹琴。
你的聪明会撞上另一个你的聪明，
在战国的乡野，在唐朝的宫廷。

已经走了那么多人，有多少人是他们自己？
但成为以前曾经有过的一个人或许有点儿可能：
比如，成为雷锋，
如果不行就成为雷锋的同事，
如果不行就成为雷锋的领导，
如果不行就成为雷锋敬重或讨厌的人，
如果不行就成为雷锋帮助过的人，
如果不行就成为雷锋读到过的人，
如果不行就成为欺负过雷锋的人，
如果不行就成为远远看见过雷锋的人，
如果不行就成为与雷锋擦肩而过的人，
如果不行就成为被雷锋事迹感动的人，
如果不行就成为质疑雷锋事迹的人，
如果不行就成为没听说过雷锋的人，
比如那些晚清的公子哥，
或者志士，或者他们的门徒，
或者他们的亲戚，或者他们的榜样——
那些更古老而你想象不出他们面孔的人。

已经走了那么多人而你想成为你自己。
我喝下你的鸡汤，赞美你的野心，
然后把这首诗读给你听。

2020.3.3

Stupid Words

I've had those stupid words "be yourself" in mind for years and I've only just
     now figured them out:
You can't really be yourself, but you can be a hundred thousand other people.
There's not a single bird that can't fly, and there's not a single monkey that can
     play piano.
Your intelligence will run into the intelligence of another you,
in the Warring States plains, or in the court of the Tang dynasty.

Many people have gone, but how many of them were ever themselves?
But it might still be possible to be someone who used to be:
for instance, Lei Feng,
and if that doesn't work then be Lei Feng's coworker,
and if that doesn't work then be Lei Feng's boss,
and if that doesn't work then be someone respected or hated by Lei Feng,
and if that doesn't work then be someone Lei Feng helped one time,
and if that doesn't work then be someone Lei Feng read about,
and if that doesn't work then be someone who bullied Lei Feng,
and if that doesn't work then be someone who saw Lei Feng from afar,
and if that doesn't work then be someone who passed right by Lei Feng,
and if that doesn't work then be someone moved by Lei Feng's deeds,
and if that doesn't work then be someone who doubts Lei Feng's deeds,
and if that doesn't work then be someone who's never even heard of Lei Feng,
like those dandies from the late Qing,
or men of integrity and ideals, or their disciples,
or their relatives, or their role models—
those people from antiquity with faces you can't imagine.

So many people have gone but you want to be yourself.
I sip your chicken soup for the soul, praise your ambition,
and read you this little poem.

March 3, 2020

2011年1月埃及纪事

见过圆明园废墟的石柱没见过卢克索神庙的石柱现在看见了。
见过两千年前的马王堆女尸没见过三千年前的拉美西斯二世现在依然没有看见。

拉美西斯二世的茉莉花不在1月开放。
茉莉花不开放，丁香花便也不开放，玫瑰花便也不开放。

拉美西斯二世没见过革命的狂欢节，
我却见证了不狂欢的革命。

1月25日。开罗。
然后卢克索。然后回到开罗。

*

卢克索神庙的石柱太粗猛，排列太密集，看不懂。常识被重塑。
好莱坞的编剧当在此幻想过外星人在外太空的军事基地。

据说每座石柱顶着五位神灵。
阿蒙神是唯一的。你真这样认为吗？

不喝水的大太阳沉入沙漠。
月照图坦卡蒙的官殿鼓励抒情的小虫子横行。

尼罗河畔以纸莎草为形象的鬼魂只要长吟便是高声长吟。

乡村。北非。阿拉伯世界。
宣礼塔上传出的歌声孤单而非个人。

出生在金字塔附近的老人，主动做拍照模特。
他向游人要钱时热情而职业，要不到钱时他的沮丧是人性的。

January 2011 in Egypt

Had seen the stone pillar ruins of Yuanmingyuan but not the stone pillars of
   Luxor Temple now I've seen them.
Had seen the two-thousand-year-old Mawangdui Marquise of Dai remains but
   not three-thousand-year-old Ramesses II now I still haven't seen him.

The jasmines of Ramesses II do not bloom in January.
When the jasmines don't bloom, the cloves don't bloom, and neither do roses.

Ramesses II never saw the carnival of revolution,
but I witnessed one that wasn't carnivalesque.

January 25. Cairo.
Then Luxor. Then back to Cairo.

*

The stone pillars of Luxor Temple are too thick and arranged too densely so I
   don't understand them. Common knowledge reconstructed.
Hollywood screenwriters imagine this as an outer space alien military base.

They say each pillar holds up five gods.
Amon is the only one. Is that really what you think?

The sun drinks no water and sinks into the desert.
The moon shines on Tutankhamen's palace encouraging lyrical insects to run wild.

On the banks of the Nile when ghosts in the form of paper reeds wail it's a
   high-pitched wail.

Desert town. North Africa. The Arabian world.
The song from the minaret is lonesome but not individual.

An old man born near the pyramids comes over to model for photographs.
Asking for money from tourists he's warm and professional, and when he doesn't
   receive anything his frustration is human.

开国八千年后人民在一团死水中挣得太少但总听说别人挣得太多。

骡马的尿骚味沿街巷飘荡。垃圾遍及旷野。
腐败的政治顾不到垃圾遍及旷野，只把厅堂收拾干净。

月工资500埃镑的中层官吏、月工资150埃镑的医生要求变革。
抱团发泄愤怒和绝望的青年互不相识。发泄了再说。

于是焚烧轮胎的黑烟升起于神庙的三面，
神庙里的诸神呛了嗓子，声称自己是外星人理应受到保护和尊敬。

惴惴不安的外国人在候机厅里吸烟没人管。
飞机上担心没处落脚的罗马尼亚姑娘后来消失于慌乱的人群。

雅娜，你在哪里？

洗劫花店的暴徒中或有一位想把玫瑰花献给心上人。
你能否成为他的心上人全看你活下来的运气如何。

中国人只进中餐馆，
在中餐馆稀有的开罗在要求变革的开罗也不例外。

中餐馆电视里一点点让步的老君王让到无步可让，
只好期待一个天才的悲剧作家将来把他写成另一个李尔王。

92

Eight thousand years after its founding the people are in a backwater earning
   too little always hearing about others making too much.

The piss stench of mules drifts through the alleys. Trash covers the wilderness.
Corrupt politics can't take care of the trash covering the wilderness; it can only
   keep the grand hall clean.

The midlevel official making E£500 a month and the doctor making E£150 a
   month demand change.
The youths banding together to vent their anger and despair don't know each
   other. Vent first, then we'll see.

So the smoke from burning tires rises from three sides of the temple,
choking the gods inside—they proclaim themselves to be aliens so they should
   get respect and protection.

Anxious foreigners are smoking in the airport waiting area and no one cares.
The Romanian girl who worried about having nowhere to put her feet later
   disappears in the chaos of the crowd.

Yana, where are you?

Among the rioters looting the flower shop may be one who wants a rose for his
   beloved.
Whether you can be his beloved depends entirely on whether you're lucky
   enough to survive.

Chinese people only go to Chinese restaurants,
no exception for a Cairo where Chinese restaurants are rare for a Cairo demanding
   change.

On the TV in the Chinese restaurant the old monarch retreats until he has
   nowhere left to retreat to,
and has to wait for a genius writer of tragedies to make him into another King Lear.

他的1973年：
西奈半岛的十月战争。埃及摧毁了以色列的巴列夫防线。

而在废黜他的2011年
开罗中餐馆饭菜的口味差到不能再差可生意照样进行。

在难民的队伍里品味革命不是请客吃饭
这已是上世纪的学问。

以巧克力充饥数次，巧克力就让人恶心。

忽然记起我走烂在长安街上的代表青春的奥胶鞋。

*

电视中的火焰。警察绿色的装甲车。
有方向而没有头脑的石头，有头脑而没有方向的人群。

枪声可以惊散三五之众，但惊不动广大的水面。
人群如大水横贯突尼斯、埃及，然后利比亚，然后叙利亚。

历史并不收容每一天。
入夜以后，解放广场上不挪脚只喘气的帐篷被收入广角镜头。

干了再说吧不知道结局。够了。
穆巴拉克在位31年。够了。他还有儿子，他还有孙子。够了。

穆斯林兄弟会的头头们连夜开会创造历史。
有人得意就有人心碎，人人心碎就不让天黑。

His 1973:
Sinai Peninsula October War. Egypt breached Israel's Bar Lev Line.

But in 2011 when he was deposed:
The food in the Chinese restaurant in Cairo was so bad it couldn't get any worse
   but business was fine.

In a crowd of refugees tasting revolution is not a dinner party
but that's something we learned last century.

Use chocolate to allay hunger enough times and chocolate becomes disgusting.

I suddenly recall the smelly rubber shoes that represent youth which I wore holes
   through on Tiananmen Square.

*

The flame on the TV. The green-armored police vehicle.
Stones with direction but no brains, crowds with brains but no direction.

Gunshot can disperse a crowd of three or five, but not a great body of water.
Like water crowds traverse Tunisia and Egypt, then Libya, then Syria.

History does not retain each day.
After nightfall, the tents on Tahrir Square gasp but do not move their feet and
   are taken in by the wide-angled lens.

We'll see after it's done no one knows the outcome. Enough.
Hosni Mubarak was in power for thirty-one years. Enough. He has sons, even
   grandchildren. Enough.

The heads of the Muslim Brotherhood have meetings all night to make history.
When some are proud some will be heartbroken, and if everyone's heartbroken
   night will never fall.

*

历史曾经终结在1989，现在再次终结在2011。
天道爱反讽。

它以后还要终结在美国、土耳其和巴西。还要终结在火星或者木星。
谁能给出个像样的解读？

人民面向现在，精英面向未来，帝王面向过去。

帝王谷墓道石壁上镂刻的《亡灵书》片段美则美矣但是看不懂。

这看不懂的法老文啊如何从尼罗河泛滥的洪水抽绎出完美的几何学？
如何表达符合星空秩序的政治学理念和必死的人生？

它有着被低估了的复杂性。
它如何调动黎明的颂神者也是傍晚的抗议者那人类的嘴唇？

美国人叫好时伊朗人也叫好。
群星后悔庇护独裁者时独裁者后悔默许了腐败的流行。

*

法老的重要性全在他们死后漫长的沉默。

我和同伴说军人的坏话时一辆满载军官的小巴士从我们身旁经过。

于是宵禁。
宵禁的意思是只许睡觉不许睡不着，或者不管睡得着睡不着必须睡觉。

History ended once in 1989, and now it's ending again in 2011.
Fate loves irony.

It will end again in America, Turkey, and Brazil. And again on Mars and on Jupiter.
Who can provide a decent explanation?

The people face the present, the elites face the future, and the kings face the past.

On the stone walls of the tomb passageway in the Valley of the Kings are carved
  excerpts from *The Book of the Dead* that are beautiful but illegible.

These illegible glyphs of the pharaohs—how was this perfect geometry deduced
  from the floods of the Nile?
How can they express a politics fitting the order of the starry sky and also mortality?

They have an underestimated complexity.
How can they mobilize dawn extollers of the gods and evening protesters the
  lips of humanity?

Americans applaud and so do Iranians.
When the constellations regret sheltering the dictator the dictator regrets
  acquiescing to the prevalence of corruption.

The importance of the pharaohs is in the length of their silence after death.

While I'm complaining about soldiers to my companion a military bus filled
  with officers passes by.

So the curfew.
Curfew means only sleep is allowed insomnia is not allowed, or you have to sleep
  whether you can fall asleep or not.

坦克车排纵队无声地进城仿佛街道上铺满了棉花。
但据我的经验，暴力的街道上本应雷声滚滚，可是不。

开罗夜色中一脸严肃的士兵英俊，廉洁，和蔼，不开枪。

他或许正是另一个年轻的穆巴拉克满怀救国理想，
难以想象自己失败的晚年。

"好男人都死在了1973年的西奈半岛，"努尔说。
穆斯林兄弟会的兄弟们宣誓要做好男人已经别无选择但也许别人不同意。

*

没赶上萨达特遇刺时的埃及赶上了穆巴拉克下台时的埃及。总会赶上点什么。
拉美西斯二世在地下庆幸荣华富贵伴随他直到漆黑的陵寝。

军队接管了国家。
不曾被预告的新时代只好匆匆开始。

各单位里砸门找头头算账的职员一个个满腔怒火和正义。

直拖到8月3日，感到委屈的穆巴拉克躺在担架上受审。
那时他已知道他的命运好于他厌恶的上校卡扎菲；

那时他已猜到
被终结的历史会一次次重新开始。

他也许哭过一次，
也许从此患上了老年痴呆症。对世事不闻不问。

2013.6.22

Tanks silently filing into the city as if the streets were paved with cotton.
According to my experience violent streets should thunder, but not here.

In the Cairo night a serious-faced young soldier is handsome, incorruptible, affable,
    doesn't shoot.

Perhaps he is another young Mubarak full of ideals about saving his nation,
unable to imagine the failures of his later years.

"All the good men died in 1973 on Sinai," Noor says.
The brothers of the Muslim Brotherhood swear there is no choice but to be a
    good man but others probably disagree.

*

Didn't make it to the Egypt of Anwar Sadat's assassination made it to the Egypt
    of Mubarak's resignation. Am always making it to something.
Ramesses II rejoices underground glory splendor wealth and rank following
    him to the dark of the mausoleum.

The army takes over the country.
An unforetold new era starts in a hurry.

At every workplace employees pound on doors looking to settle accounts with
    their bosses voices full of fury and righteousness.

Until August 3, when Mubarak feeling wronged lies down on a tank to be judged.
At least he knows he'll be better off than his nemesis Colonel Gaddafi;

he has already guessed
that an ended history will begin again, and again, and again.

Maybe he cried once,
maybe he'll get Alzheimer's. He neither hears nor asks about the news.

June 22, 2013

曼哈顿乱想
—给张旭东

终于明白，是中国人，就没办法：你头上父亲的父亲、祖父的祖父，盘旋如一架架直升机(只是没有声音)。他们追踪你来到曼哈顿，在你的头项捶胸顿足(只是没有声音)，要求你承认天使不是少年，而是老人。

老天使们吸烟，但曼哈顿吸烟的人越来越少。曼哈顿本地的少年天使认为，吸大麻比吸烟更讲究卫生，而且更前卫。对此老天使们在曼哈顿的天空破口大骂(只是没有声音)，并且吸更多的烟，好像他们但求一死。

而你不想加入天使们的争吵。这不是你的地盘。在曼哈顿，你一咕哝就变成一个清朝人，你一吐痰就变成一个明朝人。嘿，要是唐朝人来到曼哈顿，他们会给这里的年轻人一顿鞭打；而宋朝人，他们会在这里像丢江山一样丢光兜里所有的东西。

你不得不是从前曾经是过的某个人。这有点丢脸，但没人知道。没人知道你偷偷带来了一整套有关投胎转世的、未经验证的理论。这理论说：你母亲生下你，便同时也生下了你的影子你的花鸟虫鱼。

没办法，你所有的喜悦都是中国式的，你所有的愤怒都是中国式的。有时你不得不宣布：你的愤怒比中国式的愤怒更"中国"，而不是更"愤怒"。这好莱坞的游戏规则你若敢反对，你就是反对市场的铁律。

(但是在曼哈顿，人们不能区分黑龙江人的愤怒、四川人的愤怒、广东人的愤怒。人们可能会认为吴侬软语的上海人不懂得愤怒。只有西藏人的愤怒尚可理解，因为西藏人在大雪山上祈求平息他们的愤怒。)

Random Manhattan Thoughts
—for Zhang Xudong

I finally get it—if you're Chinese, there's nothing to be done: above your head, your father's father, and your grandfather's grandfather, hover like helicopters (but silently). They followed you here to Manhattan, pounding their chests and stamping their feet down your neck (but silently), demanding you acknowledge that angels are not young men, they're old men.

Old angels smoke, but there are fewer and fewer smokers in Manhattan. Manhattan's local young angels think it's more hygienic, more avant-garde even, to smoke pot than cigarettes. The old angels hurl invectives across the Manhattan sky over this (but silently), and smoke more cigarettes, as if they had a death wish.

And you don't want to get involved in the angels' argument. It's not your place. In Manhattan, just grunt and you're from the Qing dynasty, spit and you're from the Ming. Hey, if someone from the Tang came to Manhattan, they'd whip these kids for sure; and anyone from the Song would have their pockets emptied, like they were losing control of the state.

You can't help but be whoever you used to have been. This is embarrassing, but no one knows it. No one knows you're secretly carrying a ream of unproven hypotheses about reincarnation. The hypotheses say: your mother gave birth to you, and at the same time gave birth to your shadow your flowers your birds your bugs your fish.

Nothing to be done, all your joys are Chinese, all your angers are Chinese. Sometimes you have to declare: your angers aren't "angrier" than Chinese angers, but they are more "Chinese." If you dare to break these Hollywood rules of the game, you're breaking the iron law of the market.

(But in Manhattan, no one can tell the anger of people from Heilongjiang from the anger of people from Sichuan or Guangdong. People might think soft-spoken Wu dialect speakers from Shanghai don't even know how to get angry. Only the anger of Tibetans is intelligible, because Tibetans pray to quell their anger on snow-capped mountains.)

是中国人，就必须比古根海姆博物馆的后现代主义更后现代主义，比哥伦比亚大学的女权主义更女权主义，比杰姆逊脑子里的马克思主义更马克思主义；好像只有这样，才算做成了中国人。不这样行吗？不知道，在曼哈顿。

曼哈顿的雨，落在你头上只有雨水总量的千万分之一。曼哈顿的风，挤过两幢摩天大楼的缝隙，瘦成刀片，刮掉你的胡子。但是为了弄出一个"真正"的中国，你得弄出一个"伪中国"，也就是说，你得在脸上贴一片假胡子。

你得像卖咸鱼一样把你的民族主义买到世界市场，或者你得像反对咸鱼一样反对别人的民族主义。你有责任维护你苍蝇乱飞的鱼案，好像只有这样，你才能从市场管理处领到可以任你像苍蝇一样乱飞的许可证。

一个可以被分享、可以被消费的"中国梦"：一道蜿蜒在荒山秃岭间的灰砖墙、一支行进在地下的穿盔甲的大军、一座女鬼出入的大宅院、一个摇头晃脑的读书人……中国是远方一朵莲花，只适合吟诵，不适合走近。

最终，连动荡社会中的血腥之气也可以被收集加工成廉价的鼻烟，在曼哈顿的电影院里随爆米花一起成瓶销售；而大红的绸缎，既可用于婚礼，也可用于革命。依然不可理解的是为什么中国人到现在还"吃孩子"。

他们同样不能理解为什么在中国，叔叔、阿姨投胎为叔叔、阿姨，而大哥、二嫂尚未长大成人就已经做了大哥、二嫂。但你必须选择其中一个身份，选择五岁学习行酒令，八岁学习耍贫嘴，十三岁学习讲黄段子。

If you're Chinese, you must be more postmodernist than the postmodernism of the Guggenheim Museum, more feminist than the feminism at Columbia University, more Marxist than the Marxism in Fredric Jameson's brain; basically, this is the only way to be considered Chinese. Can it be otherwise? In Manhattan, I just don't know.

Manhattan rain, only one ten-millionth of the total volume of water falling on your head. Manhattan wind, squeezing through the crack between two skyscrapers, thin as a razorblade, blowing off your beard. But for there to be a "true" China there has to be a "false" China, which means you have to stick a fake beard on your face.

You have to purchase your nationalism into the world market like selling salted fish, or else you have to oppose the nationalism of others like opposing salted fish. You have a responsibility to protect your fish stand with the flies buzzing all around, as basically this is the only way you can get a permit to buzz around like flies from the market management.

A "Chinese Dream" to be shared and consumed: a wriggle of a grey brick wall atop bare mountains, an army in armor marching underground, a courtyard house with female ghosts coming and going, a scholar rocking his head back and forth . . . China is a faraway lotus, which can only be recited, never approached.

In the end, even the blood-filled air of a turbulent society can be collected and processed into cut-rate snuff, to be bottled and sold like popcorn in Manhattan movie theaters; and big red sheets of silk, they can be used in weddings or in revolutions. But what I can't figure out is why Chinese people still "eat children."

Nor can they understand why in China, aunts and uncles reincarnate into aunts and uncles, but big brothers and sisters-in-law can be big brothers and sisters-in-law even before they grow up. But you have to pick one of these identities, pick learning to play drinking games by the time you're five, learning to shoot the shit by eight, and learning to tell dirty jokes before thirteen.

最重要的是你得在学会讲黄段子的同时，学会面对土匪司令不吭一声。当土匪司令睡了大觉，也就到了你大叫大嚷的时辰。你一大叫大嚷，你的周围像换布景一样顿时耸起赌场、饭馆、旅店和洗澡堂。

2002年，秋天，曼哈顿唐人街。除了大叫大嚷你没有别的办法讲出你的心事。而神机妙算的黄大仙知道，你不曾大叫大嚷，所以你不曾讲出你的心事。所以你不一定有什么心事。唐人街上的烂虾找到臭鱼。

1911年穿马褂反对专制的中国人、1979年穿中山装花美元的中国人、2000年穿西装大嚼卤鸭子的中国人，是比中国人更伟大的中国人，因为他们长着政治的脑袋、政治的胃(而在唐人街，政治变通为花边新闻)。

波兰人、捷克人、匈牙利人、罗马尼亚人，因为有所信奉故而难以被改变面孔，但中国人难以被改变面孔是因为大家什么都不信(两者不容混为一谈)。惟一的问题是，相信一个什么都不信的人是一件困难的事。

说"是"，等于说"不是"，是难以理解的辩证法。世贸大厦并非依循这种辩证法冲到400米高空，然后化作一个虚影。说"是"等于说"不是"，是300岁的曼哈顿所不习惯的老谋深算、礼貌待人。

据说在中国，有人吸风饮露，活到700岁，真的。有人喝了符水就能刀枪不入，真的。学生们读到，车胤少时家贫，夏天以练囊集数十萤火虫照明读书。此事见载于《晋书》，所以是真的。但所有这一切合在一起便是假的。

Most important is while learning the dirty jokes, you have to learn to face the bandit chief without making a sound. When the bandit chief falls asleep, it's time to scream and shout. When you scream and shout, your surroundings will suddenly turn into towering casinos, restaurants, hotels, and bathhouses, instantaneous as a scene change onstage.

Manhattan's Chinatown, autumn, 2002. Aside from screaming and shouting you have no way to say what's weighing on your mind. But as superb strategist Wong Tai Sin knows, you've never screamed or shouted, so you've never said what was weighing on your mind. Maybe nothing is weighing on your mind. The rotten shrimp in Chinatown have found their smelly fish.

Chinese people in *magua* opposing despotism in 1911 and Chinese people in Mao coats spending US dollars in 1979 and Chinese people in business attire gnawing on stewed duck in 2000, they're all greater Chinese people than Chinese people, because they have political minds and political stomachs (and in Chinatown, politics works around gossip).

Poles, Czechs, Hungarians, Romanians, they have faith, hence their faces are hard to change, but Chinese faces are hard to change because they don't believe in anything (let's not confuse the two). The only problem is, it's hard to believe someone who doesn't believe in anything.

To say that "yes" is the same as saying "no" is a hard dialectic to follow. The World Trade Center didn't adhere to this dialectic when it grew four hundred meters high, only to become a specter. To say that "yes" is the same as saying "no" is a discretion and courtesy to which three-hundred-year-old Manhattan is not accustomed.

They say in China people breathe the wind and drink the dew and live seven hundred years—it's true. People drink a kind of elixir so knives and bullets can't pierce their skin—it's true. Students learn that one summer, when Che Yin was young and his family impoverished, he gathered dozens of fireflies into a bag to make a lamp by which he could study at night. This is recorded in the *Book of Jin*, so it must be true. But put them all together and they're false.

据说在中国，有人不用炸药、推土机，全凭意念便能将大山搬走，假的。有人在地下盖起宫殿，死后依然治理国家，假的。那避谷之人碰上个三岁小童，连忙喝下他小鸡鸡里滋出的琼浆玉液，假的吧？但所有这一切合在一起便是真的。

你假装神魔附体。靠翻白眼、吐白沫，你假装看见了前世，听懂了宇宙的福音。宇宙没有嘴巴，你假装它长了个嘴巴。你假装以宇宙为背景思念起家乡。你假装没有家乡。你假装不想。你假装不想也不行。

你假装离家七年，历尽吃喝嫖赌。你假装一辈子都耗在还乡的路上：一会儿穷，卖了宝马；一会儿富，请个菩萨与你同行；最终走进一幢房子与蝙蝠同住。你假装在这房子里睡觉，假装睡不着就吃药，假装醒不了是因为吃过了药。

你男扮女装假装死去，假装和女扮男装的人不一样。你假装梦见了天堂：不是贝亚德丽采的天堂，而是被孙猴子打烂了又修复的天堂，而是贾宝玉读到过《生死簿》的天堂。你假装在天堂里被招待了一场希腊人的锣鼓戏。

在这一刹那，曼哈顿是可以触摸的。在华尔街北边的小商店里，来自中国的T恤衫2美元一件，雨伞4美元一把，手表6美元一只。而在北京，此刻，假装到过曼哈顿的先锋派们正卖力地普及不属于曼哈顿的曼哈顿文化。

从镜子外冲到镜子里的人，有了归宿；从镜子里冲到镜子外的人，成了骗子。做一个中国人，你被规定不得不欺骗，否则你就不是一个中国人。孟德斯鸠在《论法的精神》中这样说。

They say in China they clear away mountains not with gunpowder and bulldozers but just by sheer will—that's false. Someone built a palace underground so he could continue to rule the country after death—that's false. A man who abstained from grains met a three-year-old and hurriedly gulped down all the nectar that squirted out of his pecker—that's false, right? But put them all together and they're true.

You pretend to be possessed by demons. Rolling your eyes back, frothing at the mouth, you pretend you see past lives and understand the gospel of the cosmos. The cosmos has no mouth, so you pretend it's grown one. You pretend to use the cosmos as a background to think back on your hometown. You pretend there is no hometown. You pretend not to think back on it. But you can't pretend not to think.

You pretend to be away from home for seven years, eating and drinking and gambling and whoring as much as you can. You pretend to spend your whole life on the road back home: poor, you sell your BMW; rich, you hire a bodhisattva to walk beside you; in the end, you enter a house and shelter with a bat. You pretend to sleep in this house, pretend to take pills because you can't sleep, pretend you can't wake up because of the pills you took.

You dress in drag and pretend to be dead, pretending to be different from drag kings. You pretend to have dreamt of heaven: not Beatrice's *paradiso*, but the heaven busted up and then rebuilt by the Monkey King, the heaven Jia Baoyu read about in *The Book of Living and Dying*. You pretend to have been received with a gong-and-drum play performed by Greeks.

At this moment, Manhattan is tangible. In a small shop north of Wall Street, t-shirts from China cost $2.00 per, umbrellas $4.00 each, and watches $6.00 apiece. But right now in Beijing, the vanguard who pretend to have been to Manhattan spend their energy popularizing a Manhattan culture that never belonged to Manhattan.

People who rush into mirrors from outside know a return: people who rush outside of mirrors from within become liars. Being Chinese, it's determined that you lie, otherwise you're not Chinese. Montesquieu says so in *De l'esprit des lois*.

做一个中国人，你肯定没有你的本体论、方法论。哲学是西方的概念，源自古希腊。你肯定只有一套老掉牙的、只能用来哄小孩的伦理教条。黑格尔在《哲学史讲演录》中这样说。

与此同时，你最好四大皆空或披发仗剑、修丹炼药；如果你选择背诵《四书》、《五经》，而对寒山这样的嬉皮和尚重视不够，你就是走错了道的中国人。金斯伯格在批评疯疯癫癫的老庞德时几乎这样说过。

所以中国人，这种身份，有时候是用来唬人的，有时候是用来忍气吞声的。中国的身份证不曾让你注意到身份问题；呆在家，那个"天下"里，不存在身份问题。现在，你要报名参加第56届世界身份大会。

不说yes，而说yeah，这是身份政治。而，石头什么都不说，所以石头没有身份；所以石头有时几乎不是石头，却又因此太是石头。——这是《论语》的收集者有意漏掉的夫子至言，这是中国人的秘密。

秘密。明朝王阳明在天高皇帝远的贵州龙场，在那个本不该生产思想的年头，发现任由心之所之，便可以抵达无善无恶之境。他吓得大气不敢出，赶忙用手捂住嘴，但还是汗湿了裤衩和背心。这是王阳明的秘密。

这不仅是王阳明的秘密。庄周，河南商丘的游手好闲之徒，更在两千三百年前打打杀杀的年代，与一具骷髅夜谈于河畔高丘。骷髅一开口，他便悟道，只一步就跨进了无死无生之境。这是庄周的秘密。

中国是个转椅，除了宇航员，都请上来坐坐。坐在转椅上转呀转，上即是下，左即是右，好即是坏，长即是短。这样一个国家无法对她做出准确的预言，只能说中国大概即是非中国。顺便说一句：她的诗歌大概即是非诗歌。

Being Chinese, you have no ontology or methodology. Philosophy is a western concept, originating in ancient Greece. You just have some old toothless ethical dogma good for nothing but mollifying children. Hegel says so in *Vorlesungen über die Philosophie der Weltgeschichte*.

At the same time, you'd best remain unattached to the things of this world, or untie your hair and lean on a sword, or extract medicine from cinnabar; if you decide to memorize the *Four Books* and *Five Classics*, but don't have enough respect for hippie monks like Cold Mountain, then you're Chinese but have gone the wrong way. Ginsberg almost said so in his criticisms of that old madman Ezra Pound.

So the identity of "Chinese" can be a bluff, or it can suppress indignation. Chinese ID cards never let you question identity; idle at home "under heaven" and there is no identity question. Now, you're signing up to attend the 56th Annual International Identity Convention.

To say "yeah" and not "yes" is identity politics. And since rocks can't talk, rocks don't have an identity; so sometimes rocks are barely rocks, thereby becoming too rocky—this is a saying of Confucius the compiler of *The Analects* purposely omitted: a Chinese secret.

Secret. In Longchang, Guizhou, where the mountains are high and the emperor far away, Wang Yangming in the Ming dynasty, an age that should never have produced thought, discovered that letting the heart go where it may led to a realm beyond good and evil. He gasped in fright and covered his mouth with his hands, but his pants and undershirt were still drenched in sweat. This was Wang Yangming's secret.

This wasn't only Wang Yangming's secret. Two thousand three hundred years ago, a time of viciousness and violence, an idle loafer in Shangqiu, Henan, spent all night talking to a skeleton on an embankment above the river. The minute the skeleton opened its mouth he achieved enlightenment, and he stepped into the realm beyond life and death. This was Zhuangzi's secret.

China is a swivel chair, and aside from space travelers, everyone is welcome to have a seat. Spinning on a swivel chair, up is down, left is right, good is bad, and long is short. There's no way to make an accurate prophecy for a country like this, except to say that China is probably also not Chinese. And add: her poems are probably non-poems.

但非诗歌也不是弗兰克．奥哈拉的诗歌(奥哈拉从曼哈顿的墙缝里吐出舌头)。那将李白、杜甫的诗歌背得滚瓜烂熟的人根本不懂诗歌；那将王维、寒山高抬到李白、杜甫之上的人全都毕业于曼哈顿。

曼哈顿，美国的市井，活力四射，远离仙鹤翱翔的山林水泽。所以曼哈顿人说不上优雅：吃得太多，玩得太野。而优雅的人早已于1911年死于提笼架鸟、东游西逛。这一点与其说"有诗为证"，不如说"有证为诗"。

走在曼哈顿，不做那留辫子的中国人也罢。你发现你的影子不知从何时开始剃成了光头，而且他赤身裸体，不在乎你心里中国式的害羞。你觉得这是天上那些老天使们的恶作剧；抬头望天，天上一无所有。

或许天上另有一个曼哈顿。或许曼哈顿梦想把全世界都变成曼哈顿。早晚有一天，埃兹拉．庞德漫步北京街头，会感叹"北京找不到能够称为北京的东西。"你只好劝他"再找找"，看能否发现什么秘密。

北京的秘密，就是即使北京没了城墙，没了骆驼，没了羊群，没了马粪，没了标语口号，它依然是北京。北京拆了盖，盖了拆，越拆心里越没障碍，越盖越什么都不像，但一个假北京就更是一个真北京，偏偏不是曼哈顿。

终于来到曼哈顿，早该想到的事一直不曾想到，……终于来到像一本书被划得乱七八糟的曼哈顿(一座小岛，面向大西洋)，然后带着满脑子胡思乱想回到你的大陆，喘一口气，然后从清早写到天黑。

2003.10

But non-poems don't mean Frank O'Hara's poems (O'Hara sticks his tongue out from a crack in the wall). Someone who has memorized the poems of Li Bai and Du Fu backward and forward doesn't know poetry; everyone who raises Wang Wei and Cold Mountain above Li Bai and Du Fu must have graduated in Manhattan.

Manhattan, America's central market, vibrant and dynamic, far from the mountain forests and marshlands where cranes soar. So Manhattanites aren't exactly refined: they eat too fast and play too hard. And the refined died in 1911 from hanging birdcages and traveling east and west. For this it's better not to say *there's a poem as proof*, but rather, *there's proof as a poem*.

Walking in Manhattan, you don't have to have a Chinese queue to be Chinese. You don't know when it happened but your shadow has a shaved head and is naked, caring nothing for your Chinese modesty. You figure the old angels must be playing a prank; you raise your head to look to the heavens, but there's nothing there.

Maybe there's another Manhattan up in the sky. Maybe Manhattan dreams of making the whole world Manhattan. One day, Ezra Pound will stroll through the streets of Beijing and sigh, "There is nothing in Beijing that can be called Beijing." And you'll say, "Keep looking," and see if he can discover any secrets.

Beijing's secret is: even if Beijing never had a city wall, never had camels, never had herds of sheep, never had piles of horse shit, never had slogans and political posters, it would still be Beijing. Beijing has been torn down and rebuilt, rebuilt and torn down, and the more it's torn down the less obstructed we feel, the more it's rebuilt the less it resembles anything. But a false Beijing is an even truer Beijing, because it isn't Manhattan.

Finally, in Manhattan, you never think the thing you should have thought long ago . . . you're finally in a Manhattan that's been torn to shreds like a book (a small island, facing the Atlantic), and you take all the random thoughts in your brain back to your mainland, let out a deep breath, and write from early morning until late at night.

October 2003

围海造田

围海造田之后新土地需要七年的积沉方可使用
围海造田者需要七年光阴才能安然于占领了一小片大海

这新土地上新植的树木尚未获得自然的授权
无自然授权，新树木就不会获得"树林"的感觉

飞鸟、昆虫和青蛙不愿以此为家，无论建设者怎样加班加点
海风吹过，像吹过时光停滞的停车场或者垃圾场

月照垃圾场不会比月照万里河山缺少诗意
但月照七年海滨垃圾场会让月亮的诗意获得更多的内涵

七年之痒或七年喧闹，一些看似幸福的家庭会解体
曾经相爱的人互道拜拜之后，负疚心终会接纳天高云淡

在云天之下另觅新欢的不仅是受伤的情种
做买卖、玩政治的也会从新的合伙人身上发现新的人生观

爱大笑或时常伤感的人会在七年光阴中变得麻木
而附近的街道会一直变脸，只是投机分子不会错过每一天

荀子站在新造的土地上说："人定胜天！不过，
天，需要七年光阴才会认可你围海造田"。

浮士德站在新造的土地上面对七年的荒芜忽有落寞之感
不禁抱怨起养尊处优的歌德简单理解了沧桑世变

2017.6.6

Land Reclamation

after land reclamation the new land needs seven years to settle before it can be used
the land reclaimer needs seven years just to secure a small piece of the sea

trees have not yet attained the authority of nature on this new plot of land
without natural authority, new trees do not attain the feel of a forest

birds, insects, and frogs do not want to make their homes here, no matter how
     much overtime the workers have put in
the sea breeze blows, like wind through a parking lot or garbage dump where time
     stands still

the moon shining on trash is no less poetic than the moon shining on a
     ten-thousand-mile-long river
but to shine on a seaside dump for seven years would make the moon's poetry
     more meaningful

seven-year itch or seven years of noise, some families seem happy but will break up
after people who loved each other say goodbye, all guilty hearts end up
     admitting the skies are high and the clouds are pale white

under a cloudy sky it's not just wounded romantics who seek new love
businesspeople and political types can even get another outlook on life from
     their new partners

in seven years those who love to laugh and those who get moody will all go numb
and the nearby streets will change their look, though speculators never miss a day

Xunzi stands on the new land and says: "Nature is man's to conquer! Although,
Heaven needs seven years to approve your reclamation."

Dr. Faustus stands on the new land and feels lonely in the face of seven years of
     desolation
and can't help but grumble about pampered Goethe and how simplistic his
     understanding of the vicissitudes of social change has been

June 6, 2017

金灿灿

这里，没有别的颜色只有金灿灿

金灿灿的赌场里金灿灿的宝船
金灿灿的酒店里金灿灿的狮子山

金灿灿的海上观音
保佑大街上金灿灿的金六福、周大福、周生生

金灿灿的鳄鱼在娱乐中心调戏着龙和大象
它们心甘情愿被调戏到眼冒金星好见识娱乐的金灿灿

啊，过分的金灿灿，财富的恶趣味
连垃圾桶也是金灿灿的

连太阳的金灿灿也显得暗淡
在这意识形态失踪的地方耸立着金灿灿的价值观

金灿灿的小学生们用金碗喝水
学会赌博总在无师自通手淫之前

金灿灿的男人们爱上的女人全叫"金灿灿"
可这些姑娘只会钓金鱼，养金鱼

无想象力便无性感可言
为此爱新觉罗家族绝不为公主们取名"金灿灿"

在摇曳多姿的金灿灿面前
当年曾经金灿灿的殖民者显然还不够金灿灿

他们的后代文雅、谦和
表明他们已过气，不高兴就只好滚蛋

他们上翘的嘴角，洁白的牙齿
是要证明旧殖民统治虽邪恶但品味不差对吗

Golden

here, there are no colors but golden

a golden treasure ship in a golden casino
a golden Lion Rock in a golden hotel

a golden bodhisattva on the sea
blessing golden Kin Liu Fook, Chow Tai Fook, and Chow Sang Sang on the street

a golden crocodile flirting in the entertainment center with a dragon and an
    elephant
they're happy to be hit on until golden stars fill their eyes and they see the gold
    of entertainment

oh, golden excess, wealth's malicious delight
even the trash can is golden

even the gold of the sun looks dim
where ideology has gone missing a golden value stands erect

golden grammar school students drink water from golden bowls
learning to gamble before they've mastered masturbation

golden men fall in love with women all named Goldy
but these girls only know how to fish for goldfish, to care for goldfish

no imagination, so no sex appeal to speak of
this must be why the Aisin-Gioro clan had no princesses named Goldy

before the golden sway
the golden colonists of those years don't seem golden enough

the elegance and amiability of their descendants
means that they're irrelevant, and if they don't like it they can piss off

their up-curling lips, the white of their teeth
just proves old colonial rule may have been evil but they had taste am I right

但是呸呀，现在轮到了本地人的金灿灿

谁撇嘴讥笑谁就是外人
谁就是金灿灿的反面，就是阴暗、幽暗或者黑暗

看金灿灿的资本握手金灿灿的社会福利
就是孔夫子的大同世界后来被康夫子盛赞

讲大同的他们必须热爱金灿灿
一如菩提树下饿到晕眩的王子必须热爱金灿灿

托马斯.莫尔曾设想以金链金铐锁罪犯
但乌托邦就是乌托邦啊，而金链金铐在这里并不稀罕

那么不那么金灿灿的人呢?
他们在哪里酸着像醋心偶发的知识分子?

一个酸男人朝我走来
一笑，露出颗金牙，以为我认识他

另一个酸男人也朝我走来
一笑，露出两颗金牙，问：“你梦见过我吗?”

2017.6.6

but shit, now it's time for the locals to be golden

whoever's lips curl into a sneer now is an outsider
and is the opposite of the golden, is the dull, the dim, the dark

watch golden capital give golden social welfare a golden handshake
just like the Great Unity of Confucius would later be highly regarded by Kang
    Youwei

whoever talks of Great Unity must love the golden
just like the prince starving to delirium under a bodhi tree must love the golden

Thomas More envisioned locking up prisoners in shackles of gold
but utopia is just utopia, and golden handcuffs aren't cherished here

and so what about people who aren't so golden?
where have they gone to, as sour as intellectuals suffering from heartburn?

one sour guy is walking up to me
smiling, he flashes a gold tooth, like I know him

another sour guys walks up
smiling, he flashes two gold teeth, and asks: "Have you dreamt of me?"

June 6, 2017

论读书
——仿英格.克里斯蒂安森

有的人中国书读得太多了，西方书读得太少
有的人中国书读得太少，西方书读得太多了

有的人只读西方书，但一句外语也不懂
有的人只读中国书，自号某某山人，仿佛他真住在山道的尽头

有的人中国书、西方书都读得太多，变得厌倦人世，
有的人中国书、西方书都读得太少，活在世上全靠天才和直觉

有的人没有天才和直觉也能滔滔不绝，但也没有沉默做逗号和句号
懂得使用分号和破折号的人看来不是中国人

有的人中国书、西方书都读得太多，但没读过阿拉伯和非洲的书
有的人读过几本拉丁美洲的书，但分不清那算西方书还是南方书

难道还有南方书吗?南半球的季节与北半球相反
南半球的书却不需要从最后一页读回第一页

有的人以为中国就是东方全不管印度也是东方当然它在东方的南方
而巴基斯坦和阿富汗的作家也写书尽管他们不关心孔夫子

有的人读了点书便趾高气昂了，指点江山了。江山听着
有的人读了点书便谨小慎微了，谨言慎行了，安静地喘气

On Reading
—after Inger Christensen

Some people have read too many Chinese books, too few Western books
Some people have read too few Chinese books, too many Western books

Some people only read Western books, but don't know a single phrase in
    another language
Some people only read Chinese books, and go by the alias Mountain Hermit,
    as if they lived at the end of some mountain road

Some people have read too many Chinese books and Western books, and become
    world-weary
Some people have read too few Chinese books and Western books, and live on
    nothing but their own genius and intuition

Some people with neither genius nor intuition let their words flow, but don't
    have the silence for commas or periods
People who know how to use semicolons and dashes must not be Chinese

Some people have read too many Chinese books and Western books, but
    haven't read any Arabian or African books
Some people have read a few Latin American books, but don't know for sure if
    they were Western or Southern

Are there even Southern books? In the Southern hemisphere the seasons are
    opposite than the seasons in the Northern hemisphere
But Southern books don't need to be read from the last page to the first

Some people think China is the East and don't bother thinking about India
    though of course India is the South of the East
And Pakistani and Afghani writers write books too even if they don't care
    about Confucius

Some people have read a few books and walk with their noses in the air, judging
    the rivers and mountains. The rivers and mountains are listening
Some people have read a few books and become overcautious, proper in word
    and deed, breathing quietly

有的人假装读过很多书其实是个文盲
有的人真读过很多书其实也是个文盲

有的人是真正的文盲却对读书人呼来喝去
有的人因为被呼来喝去遂愤恨地打开书本寻求真理

有的人愤恨于被呼来喝去发誓再不读书才发现大象梅花鹿从不读书
有的人一本书不读却被写进了书里而他自己不知道

有的人读书是为了寻找快乐但不是寻欢作乐
有的人寻欢作乐但书读得也不少这说明读书人并非注定清苦

有的人就把自己读瘦了头悬梁锥刺股
有的人就把自己读胖了读到满腹经纶可并不觉得肚胀

所有读书的人只会越读越老当然不读书也免不了衰老
在生死问题上读书与不读书没什么区别就像练拳不练拳没什么区别

有的人书越读越多，仿佛从河流进入大海，孤独地飘荡
有的人书读到三十岁戛然而止，然后望着大地出神到三十七岁

有的人在三十七岁告别了自己所谓天才的不着调的生活方式
坐下来，打开台灯，写书，以便将自己耗尽并且被世人忘记

有的人为书籍盖一幢房子自己只在白天进入这幽灵的房间
有的人夜间也待在幽灵的房间里但是不在其中睡觉

Some people pretend to have read a lot of books but in fact they're illiterate
Some people really have read a lot of books but in fact they're illiterate too

Some people really are illiterate but yell at people who read
Some people hate being yelled at and so pick up a book in search of the Truth

Some people hate being yelled at and so swear never to read again only to find
    out that elephants and sika deer don't read either
Some people don't read a single book but are written about in books and never
    find out

Some people read books in search of happiness but not pleasure
Some people seek pleasure but have read a number of books which means
    people who read are not in fact destined for lives of genteel poverty

Some people read themselves thin an exercise in self-flagellation
Some people read themselves fat filling their bellies and never feeling stuffed

Everyone who reads will get older the more they read of course not reading
    doesn't mean you don't age
On matters of life and death there's no difference between reading and not
    reading just like there's no difference between knowing kungfu and not
    knowing it

Some people keep on reading, drifting away in solitude, like the river flowing
    into the sea
Some people read until they're thirty and then halt, then stare at the ground in
    a daze until they're thirty-seven

At thirty-seven some people bid farewell to their genius and idiosyncratic ways
    of life
They sit down, turn on the desk lamp, and write to deplete themselves and be
    forgotten by the world

Some people build rooms for their books only going into these spectral rooms
    in the light of day
Some people spend time in these spectral rooms at night but don't sleep in
    the rooms

有的人把书从书房里扔出来腾空书房用于冥想
有的人腾空书房用于储存货物但自己也没能变成成功的商人

有的人以为腾空了书房就腾空了大脑
但大脑里总是有人哭泣有人怒吼这让他心烦意乱

有的人心烦意乱地走进书之山其实是走进了杂志之山
有的人坐在书山里不再出来是因为找不到出山的路经

有的人在书山里点火想到百年后会有人对自己痛加斥责
有的人在焚书的火焰里哈哈大笑纯粹是因为痛恨邪恶

有的人在焚书的火焰里哈哈大笑觉得这是最好的自焚
有的人认为书山当然是烧不尽的所以永生当然是可能的

有的人走出了书山剩下的时间是劝别人走进书山
有的人走出了书山对书山里的事物三缄其口

有的人对书籍说话好像作者是自己的熟人
有的人不同作者说话只是向他们鞠躬就像祭祀先祖

有的人认为尽信书不如无书这得是多牛的人啊他深入当下
有的人只信书上说的蔑视一个活生生的世界这也得自信满满

Some people throw all the books out of their libraries emptying them so they
    have somewhere to meditate
Some people empty out their libraries so they can have a place to store merchandise
    but they never become successful businesspeople

Some people think emptying out their libraries means emptying out their minds
But in their minds people are always crying people are always yelling this makes
    them depressed

When depressed some people walk into mountains of books actually they're
    mountains of magazines
Some people sit in mountains of books and never come out because they can't
    find a path out of the mountains

Some people light fires in the mountains of books thinking about how they'll
    be denounced in a hundred years
Some people burst out laughing in the flames of burning books purely out of a
    hatred for evil

Some people burst out laughing in the flames of burning books believing this is
    the best way to go up in smoke
Some people think a mountain of books will never burn up so obviously eternal
    life must be possible

Some people walk out of mountains of books and spend their remaining time
    persuading others to walk into mountains of books
Some people walk out of mountains of books and keep their lips sealed about
    what might be contained there

Some people talk to books as if the authors were their close friends
Some people don't talk to authors but bow to them as if making sacrifices to
    their ancestors

Some people think that to believe everything in books is worse than to have no
    books at all these people are awesome they fully inhabit the moment
Some people only believe what's in books scorning the living world this takes
    believing in oneself

有的人觉得三日不读书面目可憎
有的人天生丽质害怕书籍会夺走容颜

过去中国人的说法是书中自有黄金屋可现在的金价忽低忽高
而以色列的索罗门王说"积累知识就是积累悲哀"

但大人物的悲哀不是小人物的悲哀其原因不同
但读书人总是把小人物的悲哀解说等同大人物的悲哀

六朝以前的中国人就悲哀过了而且不是因为读书
宋代以后的中国人越来越爱读书但只读孔孟之书直到马列传来

有的人读书是为了最终放弃书本直至放弃自己
有的人读书在不知不觉中就变成了书虫

2016.3.8

Some people think that they look ugly if they don't read for three days
Some people have a natural beauty and fear books will steal their good looks

In the past Chinese people said in books can be found roomfuls of gold but
    now the price of gold fluctuates wildly
And King Solomon of Israel said "he that increaseth knowledge increaseth sorrow"

But the sorrow of the great is not the sorrow of the menial their causes are
    different
But people who read always explicate the sorrow of the menial as an implication
    of the sorrow of the great

Before the Six Dynasties the Chinese were sad and it wasn't due to reading
After the Song Dynasty the Chinese loved reading more and more but only
    read Confucius and Mencius until Marx and Lenin showed up

Some people read so as to abandon books in the end and so abandon themselves
Some people read books and inadvertently turn into bookworms

March 8, 2016

论高尚者

得读过几本书但不能读得太多，不能培养读书人的相对主义和犬儒主义。

在各类图书中高尚的人一般只读传记，仿佛他是要活成一本传记。

他并不非得对高尚本身感兴趣。最好的高尚是天然的高尚。但他总向高尚的前辈看齐。

他最主要的精神财富是理想主义。在理想主义的烛光面前，世界不得不暗淡。

但要谨防理想主义蜡烛的灯下黑。扑进灯下黑的飞蛾全都狡猾得不像飞蛾。

他得自觉比别人聪明，但不能聪明太多，否则就要琢磨利用别人的愚蠢。

高尚之人的隐私之一就是他的愚蠢。有时他也会显现他的愚蠢但并非故意出丑。

或许他得既聪明又愚蠢，但不能是小聪明和小愚蠢。

要玩就玩大的：他得挑大个的西瓜，爬大个的山。他得欣赏大个的月亮。

对他来说天道不证自明。他自觉有资格代天说话，这也是不证自明的。

要是使命感像发烧一样发作，他会烧成一个滚烫的英雄。

在拿不准真善美的准确定义的情况下，他得高歌真善美。做个反智主义者。

反智主义者统统认为道德天成，但有时，他又会犹豫该否为高级道德去牺牲低级道德。

On the Noble

They have to have read some books but can't have read too much or they'll take on the relativism and cynicism common to readers.

In books of all kinds the noble tend to read biographies, like they're trying to live themselves into biographies.

They don't have to be interested in nobility *per se*. The best nobility is a natural nobility. But they always emulate the nobility of their elders.

Their main source of spiritual wealth is their idealism. Before the candlelight of idealism, the world cannot but darken.

But beware the darkness beneath the candlelight of idealism. Moths that fly into this darkness become so cunning they're no longer moths.

They must consciously be more intelligent than others, but not too intelligent or they will start considering how to take advantage of others' stupidity.

One of the secrets of the noble is their stupidity. They may reveal their stupidity at times but they never make a fool of themselves deliberately.

They may be both stupid and intelligent, but cannot be clever and foolish.

If you're going to play, play big: they pick big watermelons, climb big mountains. They bask in the light of big moons.

For them the truth is held to be self-evident. Consciously they are qualified to speak for truth, which is itself self-evident.

If a sense of mission rises like a fever, they will burn like a boiling hero.

In the absence of a precise definition of truth, goodness, and beauty, they will sing the praises of truth, goodness, and beauty. As an anti-intellectual.

Anti-intellectuals all believe morality is natural, but at times they may be undecided about whether to sacrifice high morals for low ones.

难道道德是分层的吗?道德若分层,那阴曹地府是多少层?天堂又是多少层?

对此他不置可否。他低下头。他不是装傻,他是拿不准。

他肯定得有些童心啦至少在别人看来。童心可保证一个人的透明。

他不一定总是性情的啦至少在别人看来。哪有高尚的人不着四六?

如果他干了什么不妥的事,他得有高尚的借口。他得自我说服,咽回自己的唾沫。

他为社会的不公,为受到伤害的人们哭泣,有时也为无家可归的小猫小狗流眼泪。

但他不能探讨邪恶。他回避邪恶。无论是外在的还是内在的,黑色的还是白色的。

他有时会遭到来自他自己灵魂的严肃打击。这时他才知道他是有灵魂的。

这时哭是没用的。哭得再长久,再好看,再感人也没用。别指望魔鬼的善心。

在此情况下他得依然坚持一个淡淡的我,好赶走身后自私自利的大狗熊。

他得给欲望剪枝,却给爱浇水,这矛盾啊,是高尚的矛盾。

在诱惑的花园他不能逗留,在恐惧的房间他得自信刀枪不入,百毒莫功。

Are there levels to morality? If so, then on what level is the underworld? On what level heaven?

They say nothing of this. They lower their heads. They're not acting dumb, they're just unsure.

They definitely exhibit a certain childlike innocence at least in the eyes of others. Innocence proves a person's transparency.

They may not always be temperate at least in the eyes of others. Where are there nobles who are eccentric?

If they do something inappropriate, they must have a noble excuse. They must convince themselves, swallowing their own saliva.

They shed tears over the social injustices of society for people who have been hurt, at times even for homeless cats and dogs.

But they cannot investigate evil. They avoid it. Whether it be internal or external, black or white.

They may suffer attacks that come from their own souls. Only at such times do they know they have souls.

At such times crying is of no use. However long they cry, however good they look, however moving it may be—useless. Don't count on sympathy from the devil.

In such cases they must maintain indifference to keep the black bears of selfishness behind their backs at bay.

They must prune the branches of desire, yet water love—a contradiction that is a noble contradiction.

They must not linger in the garden of seduction, must remain confident of their invulnerability in the chamber of fear, confident that one hundred poisons could not succeed.

如果他心生哀愁那也只能是淡蓝色的，如五四之后第一拨文艺青年。

他得表达他的原谅如高层民国范儿。但这不妨碍他有时背后骂人如60年代的受气包。

他得善待小人直到忍无可忍，甩他一嘴巴，然后内疚，内疚，直到另一个小人出现。

谦虚的自我高估是必要的。由于这一点他不与俗人为伍。他只好与自己为伍。

高尚的人难免孤独，但他从不是自己的陌生人。他从不叫自己大吃一惊。

他往往是某种意义上的旁观者，因为旁观者总是干净的，如尚未拆封的书籍。

他站在雨里、雪里，主动或者被动。被动的旁观者中高尚者居多。

可是高尚者也不能过于高尚。比高尚还高尚的要么是神要么是伪君子。

他不能计较小恩小惠。他得大度如江湖大哥。所以他发光，甚至发福。

他不能计较小恩小惠，还得经常献出自己，好理解"奉献"这个词的基本含义。

他不需要被掌声鼓励。但有掌声更好。就像晴朗的天空飘几朵白云更美丽。

他得能够欣赏美丽的世界，哪怕它略显俗气，但理解崇高，说不上！

他得具备触景生情的能力，回忆的能力，展望未来的能力，但可能有一个坏记性。

If their hearts yield to grief, it is a pale blue grief, like the first batch of arts students after May 4, 1919.

They have to express forgiveness like high-level sophisticates of the Republican Era. But that won't keep them from sometimes cursing people behind their backs like punching bags in the sixties.

They must be kind to the petty until they can't bear it, chew them out, then feel guilty about it until another petty person comes along.

Humble overestimation of themselves is essential. Because of this they do not associate with most people. They only associate with themselves.

The noble can't avoid loneliness, but they are never strangers to themselves. They never leave themselves surprised.

They are usually spectators to some degree, because the spectator is always clean, like a book that hasn't been unwrapped.

They stand in the rain or snow, actively or passively. Most passive spectators are noble.

But the noble cannot be too noble. More noble than the noble are either gods or charlatans.

They can't quibble over small favors. They must be as magnanimous as mobsters. So they glow, even gain weight.

They can't quibble over small favors, and must often give of themselves, so as to understand what *dedication* really means.

They do not need the encouragement of applause. But it's better to have it. The way a clear sky becomes more beautiful with some drifting.

They need to know how to appreciate beauty in the world, even if they come off as uncouth, but as for understanding the sublime—not really!

They have to be ready with nostalgia, with recollections, and with gazing into the future, but they may have short memories.

他可能是过去的人或者未来的人。至于是不是现在的人他没想过。

没想过现在的含义，但他得爱家人、朋友，甚至陌生人，至于是否要爱自己他只能顺其自然。

他的爱只能与小数额的钱财挂钩。他得相信太多的钱财会像大铁炉子熔化高尚。

为避免做秀的感觉他得成为只拥有小数额钱财的众人，得是一只高尚的羊走在羊群中间。

他从不斜视，偷看他人。他看你时他的脸迎着你。他的真诚只有正面没有侧面。

即使在暗夜里他也只有正面形象。只在这一点上他注重形象问题。正面照镜子最方便。

与别人不同，高尚者会在镜子里照出自己的前世，别人只能照出容貌。

在这一点上高尚者保留了一点点古朴的神秘主义。尽管他也许不承认。

具有神秘主义倾向的高尚者常常发出耸听的危言，但往往无效。

那为什么要高尚呢? 为了尊严吗? 为了安心吗? 为了愉快吗? 一定有些好处。

做一个高尚的人，世界跟他过不去时他跟这世界死磕。

2017.7.15

They may be from the past or the future. As for whether they're from the present, well, they've never thought about that.

They've never thought about the meaning of the present, but they must love their family and friends, and even strangers, though as to whether or not they love themselves they'll follow nature's course.

Their love can only be tied up with small amounts of money. They need to believe too much money would smelt their nobility like a furnace.

To avoid the sense of putting on a show they must become part of the crowd of people with a small amount of money, must be a noble sheep walking among a herd of sheep.

They never sneak sideways glances at anyone. When they look at you they face you full on. The face of their sincerity has only a front and no profile.

Even in the darkness of night they appear to only have a front. This is the only time they are concerned with appearances. The best way to look in a mirror is straight on.

Unlike everyone else, when the noble look in mirrors their reflections are their past lives, while everyone else sees their faces.

In this respect the noble have maintained a touch of quaint mysticism. Though they probably won't admit it.

The noble with mystical tendencies are prone to overstatement but usually to no effect.

So why be noble? For dignity? For peace of mind? For happiness? It must bring some benefit.

To be noble, when the world is against them, they fight a death match against the world.

July 15, 2017

不要剥夺我的复杂性

既不要从右边剥夺我，也不要从左边剥夺我；既不要为我好而剥夺我，也不要为我更好而剥夺我。

剥夺我我就叫疼而这还是好的。

如果你剥夺一朵花的复杂性它就死掉；如果你剥夺一座坟墓的复杂性比如抽走一块墓砖，它就给你垮掉，将你捂死在别人的墓穴。

我看似简单但我其实复杂，像蚊子一样比深蓝计算机更复杂。

大象明白这个道理，从不否认蚊子的复杂性，所以它对钻进耳朵讲下流故事的蚊子毫无办法。

下流的蚊子像知识分子一样复杂，所以保持着知识分子那或真或假的独立立场，这本身已足够复杂。

虽然蚊子寿命短暂但它依然是大自然的一部分——你请消灭蚊子试试看。你敢否认大自然的尊严那也请试试看。

大自然通过保持复杂性而保持尊严——我也一样。

所以别拔我的羽毛，别改我的日历，别撕我的日记本。

我生在革命的1963年。不要把我剥夺成一个只会说NO的傻瓜。我曾在1980年代死里逃生。不要把我剥夺成一个不会说NO的傻瓜。

也不要把我剥夺成一个英雄；

也不要以为英雄总是站在剥夺者一边或剥夺者的对立面；也不要以为英雄不复杂，就像凡夫俗子并非不复杂。

Don't Deprive Me of My Complexity

Don't deprive me from the right, and don't deprive me from the left; don't deprive me for my own good, and don't deprive me for anything better.

Deprive me and I'll scream it hurts and that's a good thing.

If you deprive a flower of its complexity it will die; if you deprive a grave of its complexity by, for example, removing a clay brick it will collapse, suffocating you in someone else's grave.

I may seem simple but I'm complex, the way a mosquito is more complex than Deep Blue.

Elephants understand this logic, and so never deny the complexity of mosquitoes, even if this means they have to listen to the dirty stories those insects buzz in their ears.

Dirty mosquitoes are as complex as intellectuals, so they take the stance—perhaps real, perhaps fake—of independent intellectuals, which is complex enough on its own.

Although the lifespan of mosquitoes is short, they're part of nature—just try to get rid of them. If you want to deny the dignity of nature, just try.

Nature retains dignity by retaining complexity—same as me.

So don't pluck my feathers, don't change my calendar, and don't tear up my diary.

I was born in the revolutionary year of 1963. Don't deprive me like some idiot who can only say no. I barely made it through the 1980s with my life intact. Don't deprive me like some idiot who can't say no.

And don't deprive me like a hero;

and don't assume the hero always stands with the depriver, or always against the depriver; don't assume the hero isn't complex, just as the average person may be complex.

当你想要一个真实我给你一个虚构；当你想自我虚拟我用一把钉子钉住你的双脚在大地上。

我在1992年变成五个我：苦涩的我、怀疑的我、不确定的我、笑出声来的我，以及行舟于汹涌冷酷的历史之河的我。

所以在2011年我认定将世界区分为黑白两造的人缺心眼。

连黑白照相机都能容纳灰色，更别说擅于分辨浩荡秋天十万种色彩的我。

公鸡不打鸣时我打鸣。

不要把我剥夺成一只公鸡；更不要以为你剥夺了我就剥夺了公鸡的复杂性。为了保持公鸡的复杂性请不要剥夺我的复杂性。

我复杂因为四周的鸟雀和走兽是复杂的。

我复杂但现在我累了，愿意暂且闭嘴。我闭嘴但依然复杂。本诗到此结束。

2011.12.20
孟买

When you want reality I'll give you fiction; when you want a virtual you I'll nail both your feet to the ground.

I turned into five of me in 1992: the bitter me, the suspicious me, the uncertain me, the me who laughs out loud, and the me who navigates the cold and turbulent river of history.

So in 2011 I became determined that those who divide the world into black and white are just obtuse.

Even a black-and-white camera can accommodate grey, not to mention someone like me, who can make out the hundred thousand mighty colors of autumn.

When the rooster doesn't crow, I crow.

Don't deprive me like a rooster; and don't assume that by depriving me you can deprive a rooster of its complexity. Don't deprive me of my complexity so you can deprive a rooster of its complexity.

I am complex because all the birds and beasts around me are complex.

I am complex but right now I'm tired, and would like to shut up for a while. I'm shutting up but am still complex. And here this poem ends.

December 20, 2011
Mumbai

口罩颂

要是有可能，我会戴着口罩走进沙漠去会见天仙和天使。

我戴口罩抗拒沙尘暴，戴口罩抗拒雾霾，戴口罩捱过禽流感的日子、非典的日子、新冠病毒的日子。老舟已过万重山，后面还是万重山！

我也曾为赶时髦戴口罩，为显身份戴口罩，为躲监控戴口罩，为高喊也为自言自语戴口罩。我的口罩生涯已如古人的无口罩生涯一般绚烂！

但我还没疯到要去抢银行。但口罩自有疯劲儿和蛮力，银行职员们最好戴口罩以回击，用明亮的眼神去战胜眼神浑浊、慌乱、恶狠狠的抢劫犯。

新时代的他人，那些网络喷子，应该也是戴口罩的。匿名发言就是戴口罩发言。如果他们口罩、墨镜全戴上，他们就是黑客的跟班，等着被封号。

但说到底，除了医生、护士，戴口罩的都是胆小良民，口罩保护他们的瑟瑟发抖。你看电影里的黑帮从不戴口罩。他们老派的帅气为警察省事。

胆小良民们给狗戴上口罩，给猫戴上口罩，并且梦想着给老鼠、蝙蝠和穿山甲也戴上口罩。不得不说，这是超现实主义诗歌所扎根的现实！

超现实主义诗歌胜利的节点是：戴口罩吃饭，戴口罩抽烟喝酒，戴口罩做爱，戴口罩吐痰，戴口罩死去。超现实主义者们死灰复燃了一次次。

老妈从柜子里翻出口罩让我戴上。她因勤俭持家、杜绝浪费的好习惯，无意间保存下来这些口罩，来自十七年前的非典时期。

Ode to Facemasks

If I could, I would put on a facemask and walk into the desert to meet with fairies and angels.

I put on a facemask to resist sandstorms, put on a facemask to resist smog, put on a facemask to make it through days of the avian flu and days of SARS and days of the novel coronavirus. The old boat has passed ten thousand mountains, but there are another ten thousand mountains before me!

I've worn a facemask to be fashionable, worn a facemask for my identity, worn a facemask to avoid the mass surveillance system, and worn a facemask to shout and to talk to myself. My tenure wearing facemasks is just as glorious as the tenure of those in antiquity who didn't have facemasks!

But I haven't gone so crazy I'd rob a bank. Facemasks have a certain insanity and brute force, though, so bankers should fight back with their own facemasks and their bright eyes will triumph over the blurry, bewildered, brutal eyes of the robbers.

Others of the new era, those internet trolls, are probably wearing facemasks too. To post anonymously is to post while masked. If they put on sunglasses along with their facemasks, they'll be footmen to hackers, waiting to be crowned with blocked accounts.

But after all, from doctors and nurses, people wearing facemasks are just scared citizens, facemasks protecting their trembling. The gangsters you see in movies never wear facemasks. They save the cops a lot of trouble with their old-school good looks.

Scared citizens put facemasks on their dogs, put facemasks on their cats, even dream of putting facemasks on pangolins and mice. I have to say, this is the reality surrealist poetry is rooted in!

The node of surrealist poetry's victory is: wear a facemask to eat, wear a facemask to smoke or drink, wear a facemask to make love, wear a facemask to spit, wear a facemask to die. The surrealists come back to haunt us again and again.

Mom dug through the cupboard in search of facemasks for me to wear. Since she keeps a tidy house and hates to waste anything, she had unintentionally kept a stash of facemasks for seventeen years, ever since the SARS crisis.

我对老妈说：你看口罩已断货，我真后悔没事先开个口罩厂来大赚一笔。我为我对社会、经济和历史生活的缺乏理解而懊丧了一星期。

但一星期过后我自认为加深了对于命运的认识，遂决心在药店恢复口罩供货以后开始囤积口罩，并因此不道德地盼待下一个口罩季。

有中国人因戴口罩而在悉尼街头挨打，被柏林警察要求摘下口罩。光嘴儿的悉尼人、柏林人哪能理解，这是我们的生活习惯和存在方式！

要是有可能，我会光着屁股带着口罩走进沙漠去会见天仙和天使。

别人认不出戴口罩的我，我因戴口罩也认不出自己。我在心里一遍遍确认我是谁，但总被口罩坚决否认。但其实我摘下口罩时，它什么也不是。

2020.2.26

I said to her, Now that facemasks are out of stock, I can't believe I didn't open a facemask factory back when I had the chance—I'd be rich! I spent a whole week lamenting my lack of understanding of society, economics, and history.

But after a week I figured my understanding of fate had deepened, so as soon as the drugstores were selling facemasks again I started stockpiling them, unethically looking forward to the next facemask season.

There have been Chinese people getting beaten up on Sydney streets for wearing facemasks, or ordered to remove their facemasks by the police in Berlin. How can the naked mouths of Sydney and Berlin understand? This is our way of life and means of existence!

If I could, I would put on a facemask and walk bare-assed into the desert to meet with fairies and angels.

People don't recognize me in a facemask, and because I wear a facemask I don't recognize myself. In my own mind, I confirm who I am over and over, but my facemask always denies me. And yet, when I take off my facemask, it turns out to be nothing.

February 26, 2020

好好

好好,我不打喷嚏,不咳嗽,我一个月以后再打,再咳;如果一个月以后还不允许,那我就再推迟一个月。总之我是要把喷嚏打出来的,把咳嗽咳出来的。老天爷,你不让我打,你不让我咳,我顾全大局,但你得知道你欠了我的情。你已经欠我很多情了。

好好,我不传播小道消息。为了不传播小道消息我曾经把耳朵塞上,把眼睛闭上,但因为同时也无法听到、看到那总是慢一拍的大道消息,我又从耳朵里取出塞子,睁开眼睛。如果我说得不对,老天爷,那你就赏我个官做做,咱也好有机会高瞻远瞩。

好好,我不死,我也不让我的家人、朋友、同事死。我给他们逐一打电话。他们问我是否有事想不开。他们要冒生命危险来看我。我说没事没事,就是有事我也更有觉悟。他们于是就更不放心了。我于是只好出门去看他们,仿佛街道是别人的,咱只是偶然用一下。

各种谎话说过之后,我成功办下许多出门证,记住了许多小区的暗号。我看到朋友、同事们在发呆,在玩手机,在唱歌,在做饭,在写诗;他们拒见我时就是在做爱。我隔门提醒他们:做爱可以但不能色情。那些盯着疫情进展的官眼也盯着舆情和色情的进展。

好好,我不添乱。我整理好书架,擦干净桌椅,给窗台上的花卉消毒,给猫讲故事。我收起思绪,收起好奇心,找出多年前藏在鞋柜里的一对翅膀。抱歉,老天爷,我要起飞了!我至少要在青天里飞一会儿!不过起飞之前我要减肥,清肺,灌肠,照下镜子。

All Right, All Right

All right, all right, I won't sneeze, I won't cough, I'll wait a whole month before sneezing or coughing; if I'm still not allowed to sneeze or cough in a month, then I'll put it off for another month. But at some point I'm going to have to sneeze, going to have to cough. If you don't let me cough or sneeze, dear God, I'll try to take the whole situation into account, but you'll owe me one. You owe me so much already.

All right, all right, I won't spread rumors. To keep from spreading rumors I once plugged my ears, shut my eyes, but then I couldn't hear or see the proper truth, which always comes a beat too slow, so I unplugged my ears and opened my eyes. If I say something wrong, dear God, then give me a position in government— we'll have a chance to take the long view.

All right, all right, I won't die, and I won't let my family, friends, or coworkers die. I call each one up. They ask me if I'm all right. They want to come see me, even if it means risking their lives. I say it's nothing, it's nothing, it's just that I've had my consciousness raised. After which they get even more worried. So I have to go out and see them, as if the streets belonged to someone else, and I just happened to be passing through.

After all sorts of lies, I finally manage to get my hands on the exit permits, and remember the secret codes of various neighborhoods. I find my friends and coworkers in a daze, playing on their cellphones, singing, cooking, writing poems; whenever they refuse to see me I know they're making love. I remind them from the other side of the door: making love is fine but no porn! The eyes keeping track of the spread of the pandemic are also keeping track of public opinion and the spread of pornography.

All right, all right, I won't cause trouble. I straighten the bookshelves, wipe down the table and chairs, disinfect the flowers on the windowsill, tell stories to the cat. I put away my thoughts, put away my curiosity, and dig out that pair of wings I had hidden in the shoe cabinet all those years ago. Sorry, dear God, I have to fly! I need to fly for just a little while at least in the clear blue sky! But before takeoff I need to lose some weight, clear my lungs, have an enema, and look in the mirror.

背负青天朝下看，不得不说，我爱这人间城郭。我只说自己的坏话不说人间的坏话。我爱这有点儿慌张、有点儿幽默，有点儿粗俗的人民，尽管多数时候我也是人民中的一个。人人逗乐在疫情传播的时候，除了那些连医生也救不了的要死之人——

他们从未为死亡做好准备。

2020.2.28

Looking down with the blue sky at my back, I have to say, I do love this city and all its people. I've just been badmouthing myself, not the whole human world. I love these people, as flustered and funny and vulgar as they can be, even though most of the time I am one of them. Everyone is making fun of this pandemic, except for all the people dying because even doctors can't save them—

they never prepared for death.

February 28, 2020

絮叨，或思想汇报

舞台服装不是用来谈恋爱的，军装不是用来登上舞台的。

一个人可以狂喜但无法狂欢，几个人或许有可能欢娱至狂。

欢娱至狂的夜晚，臭味儿相投的男女斗舞在一起，缠扭在一起，

灯灭灯开，忽然来了一个没有臭味儿的人。

为了加入，他撕个布条写上"臭味儿"绑上头。——本来是娱乐，搞得像要拼命。

OK，入场吧。保罗.麦卡锡式的呕吐、流眼泪流鼻涕，拉屎撒尿并虚脱……

比愚蠢更愚蠢的是重复的愚蠢。奶子逼近奶油的麻木。玩不出新花样。

再端上桌来的是晕菜。尖叫和咆哮遭遇新时代的美丽。

看看看看这花样的女人下流到开花，下流出反抗。

为狂欢而狂欢相当于为艺术而艺术。好样的。但作死的病人不值得同情。

这上百年的真理也许背后是上千年的理由。

上千年打呼噜的睡眠和安静的睡眠统统梦到今天……

但地球撞地球，玩不出新花样。让人厌倦。

_____

Loquaciousness, or: Thought Report

Stage costumes aren't meant for courtship; military uniforms aren't meant for wearing onstage.

A person can be ecstatic but not in ecstasy, while a few people might be able to exult.

On an exultant night, a man and woman who don't pass the smell test dance together, get entangled with each other,

then the lights flicker and someone who does pass the smell test suddenly appears.

To join in, he tears off a strip of a cloth on which he's written "smell test" and ties it around his head. —It started in good fun, but now it's a fight to the finish.

Okay, he's in. Vomiting, tears in his eyes, nose running, shitting and pissing and collapsing like Paul McCarthy . . .

More stupid than stupidity is repeated stupidity. Milk approaching the numbness of cream. No new tricks to play.

The next bite to take is more than you can chew. Screaming and howling meet the beauty of the new age.

Look look look look at this blooming woman so blue she blossoms go blue in resistance.

To be ecstatic for ecstasy's sake is like art for art's sake. Good job. But sick people looking for death deserve no sympathy.

Behind this century of truth may be a millennium of reason.

A millennium of snoring sleep and quiet sleep all dream of today . . .

But when the earth crashes into the earth, there are no new tricks to play. It gets wearisome.

———————————————

仅仅是浩叹，没有意义。即使是神秘的浩叹，也没有意义。

没有上下文的鬼画符。吓唬鬼吗？鬼老练到不吃这一套。

突然的闪光。头头是道的雄文，又是浩叹。吓唬谁？

煞有介事的呼吸、愤青的记忆，即使来自心灵，也是假的。

黑暗在河流上飘荡，不是真的。太阳变黑，不是真的。

超现实主义修辞，满足超现实主义臆想。意外。诗的诞生。好样的。

但超现实主义形而上学的死亡，不是真的。

没有留下尸体的死亡，传说而已。满足了修辞的勃起。

太平间里的安静不同于荒野中的安静。

———————————————

满耳道听途说的真理，满脑子道听途说的主义，这怎么行？

黑道大哥干上了主义才是真牛逼。

是酒后胡言过分地取用了哲学语调，被康德和黑格尔取笑为诗。

被庄子和列子取笑为哲学。

被我取笑为野生哲学；其定义是：没有谱系的高谈阔论。

谁敢蔑视直觉啊，那蛮不讲理的东西，伟大的骗子！

Just letting out a deep sigh is pointless. Even if it's a mysterious deep sigh, it's still pointless.

Illegible cursive. A curse? The accursed are too sophisticated for that.

A sudden flash. A masterpiece of argumentation, but also a deep sigh. Who are you cursing?

A display of breathing and angry youths' memories, even if from the soul, are fake.

Darkness drifting along the river, it's not real. The sun going black, it's not real.

Surrealist rhetoric fulfils surrealist illusions. An accident. The birth of poetry. Good job.

But the death of surrealist metaphysics, it's not real.

Death that doesn't leave behind a corpse, it's just a myth. Fulfilling rhetoric's erection.

The quiet of the morgue is different from the quiet of the wilderness.

Ears full of hearsay truth, brain full of hearsay isms, how's that going to work?

The mafioso who can take out a hit on an ism is the real made man.

It's the drunken nonsense taking too philosophical a tone that was mocked by Kant and Hegel for being poetry.

And mocked by Zhuangzi and Liezi for being philosophy.

And mocked by me for being feral philosophy; definition: diatribes without pedigree.

Who would dare despise intuition, that thing beyond reason, that great liar!

而民间诗歌不好也得好，并不好在"诗歌"，而是好在"民间"。

民间哲学与民间科学同源而互不搭理。

思想在刀片上照镜子。深藏不露的人最好保持深藏不露。

否则丢人现眼。——那就把丢人现眼进行到底！

活成深渊不理解活成高峰的含义。平原上适合说风凉话。

深渊对覆雪的高峰展开诋毁。

———————————————————

心，人人都有。心灵，仿佛是另外的东西。

心灵从不患心脏病吗？心灵搞不懂心灵自己。

心灵是用来回归的吗？——这么多年来你都在哪里？

回归心灵而心灵是什么？是初念？是初中生羞红的脸？

回归一片虚无就能沐浴万丈光芒吗？就能真理在握吗？

家园据说也是用来回归的。回归而后盘踞。吓唬谁？

没有回归就没有家园吗？家园里有四季吗？

Poetry of the people is good even when it's no good, not necessarily as poetry, but for being of the people.

Philosophy of the people and science of the people spring from the same source, but pay each other no heed.

Thought looks in the mirror on the blade of a knife. People who conceal themselves had better stay concealed.

Unless they embarrass themselves—in which case they should embarrass themselves all the way through!

Life as an abyss will never understand life as a peak. The plains are a good place to shoot the breeze.

The abyss denigrates snow-covered peaks.

———————————————————

Everyone has a heart, but the soul seems to be another matter.

Can the soul get a heart attack? The soul doesn't understand itself.

Is the soul something to go back to? —Where have you been all these years?

Back to the soul, but what is the soul? First thought? A blushing face in junior high?

Can returning to nothingness bathe you in ten thousand rays of light? Can you grasp the truth?

They say home is what you go back to. Gone back to and seized. Who are you trying to curse?

If there's nowhere to go back to is there then no home? Are there four seasons at home?

有怕冷的爹娘吗?可以撒个娇吗?家园里长草吗?

蝴蝶双飞西园草。愁死个望夫的小妮子!

这这这是什么不刮风不下雨的所在?

———————————————————

当悲观主义成为意识形态的时候真正的悲观主义者感到不好意思。

选择成为乐观主义者被领导喜欢,被同伴们唾弃。

那些哈哈大笑的悲观主义者,那些功成名就的悲观主义者,

怎么好意思继续悲观下去?仿车尔尼雪夫斯基问题:怎么混?

T.S.艾略特不用化妆也是悲观主义者,被伍尔夫发现了小秘密。

倪瓒浑身扑香水被张世信在太湖的游船上痛打一顿而不出声。

"出一声就俗了",他说。他宁要一个烂屁股。

但烂屁股超越于悲观主义之上。当世界真的陷于悲惨。

悲观主义盛行于不那么悲惨的时代。

悲观主义的女神进不了油腥的厨房。

悲观主义的女神,一个咬着嘴唇的大影子,高高在上。

———————————————————

Are there parents afraid of the cold? Can you act spoiled? Does grass grow at home?

The paired butterflies over the grass in the west garden. Worried sick about her
    husband, a girl climbs the lookout.

What what what is this this place of no wind no rain?

When pessimism becomes an ideology true pessimists are embarrassed.

Choosing to be optimists they're liked by their leaders but scorned by their peers.

Those pessimists laughing their heads off, pessimists full of success and
    accomplishment,

but how could they feel right staying so pessimistic? As Chernyshevsky asked:
    What is to be done?

T. S. Eliot didn't need makeup to be a pessimist, and Woolf found out his little
    secret.

Ni Zan doused himself in perfume and was beaten up by Zhang Shixin on a
    cruise ship on Lake Tai, but he didn't make a sound.

"Make a sound and you're vulgar," he said. He'd rather have his ass beaten.

But a beaten ass surpasses pessimism. When the world has truly fallen into misery.

Pessimism prevails in times of lesser misery.

The goddess of pessimism cannot enter a greasy kitchen.

The goddess of pessimism, a big shadow biting her lip, up up on high.

曾经，思慕远方就拿苏联黄毛作为西方黄毛的替代品；

在两种黄毛都没有时，就拿少数民族作为异域风情的替代品。

曾经和现在，小道消息替代真相传布于居民楼和大街小巷，润色着生活。

的确凉曾经替代棉布，现在棉布唱着自然的高调又冲了回来。

现在，电视中、网络上、舞台上的爱情故事或许是政治生活的替代品，

而娱乐明星们不是或许是而是肯定是替代了画中人。

哑巴急了大吵大闹，能一下子替代健全人的低声细语。

录音机只要有电就能没完没了地替代真嗓子推销商品。

在没有田园时以荒原和农家乐作为替代品，可也。

而被替代的生活也是生活。闭嘴！

试过了: 半是真诚半是逞能的高音歌唱。

试过了: 狮子、老虎的中音还有高压电塔上变压器的低音，

也试过停电时灯泡的沉默。

想起李太白的拔剑四顾心茫然。

Once, admiring from afar, I took a child from the Soviet Union as a substitute for a child from the west;

when neither youngster is around, you can use ethnic minorities as a substitute for the exotic.

Once as well as now, rumors substitute for truth in residential buildings and on avenues and down alleys, adding finishing touches to life.

Coolness did once substitute for cotton, and now cotton comes rushing back singing in its natural high pitch.

Maybe now romances on TV, online, and onstage are substitutes for politics,

but not just maybe it definitely is the case that celebrities are substitutes for figures in paintings.

A deaf-mute getting upset and raising a ruckus can substitute for the whispers of the non-disabled.

As long as a tape recorder has batteries it can substitute for a real throat hawking goods into perpetuity.

When there are no fields or gardens, uncultivated wilderness and rural tourism can substitute, that's all right.

Life that's been substituted is still life, though. Shut up!

———————————————————

Attempted: singing falsetto, half sincere, half bravado.

Attempted: lion and tiger alto, and transformer tenor on a high-voltage tower,

as well as an attempt at lightbulb silence in a power outage.

I thought of Li Bai drawing his sword and looking around, at a loss.

试过了：大抒情、小抒情、大叙事、小叙事，

伴随着尖叫、呻吟以及洋洋自得的高潮般的胡言乱语。

不高潮的小孩子们给星星、山峰与河流命名。

中年人一边爱自然，一边在自然中耍横，

一边与人民打成一片，一边不与人民打成一片，忘了自己也是人民。

一家小书店高中毕业的小老板忽然抓住我的胳膊说：

"我认出来了，你是一个理想主义者！"

一个理想主义者飞翔，潜水，坐在树下发呆，看雨落下，

跟死人说话，屏蔽所有活人的声音，

拉上窗帘，自造一个黑盒子，自造一个宇宙，

然后 想起李太白的拔剑四顾心茫然

喜鹊写了本书而乌鸦也写了本书。

喜鹊听不懂乌鸦的话只好请麻雀做翻译。

只要说话就得有翻译。聋子省了多少事！

青蛙用20种方言聒噪。动物之间相互咒骂说脏话吗？

只要有爱就有咒骂和脏话。没有咒骂和脏话的地方没有爱。

Attempted: great lyricism, minor lyricism, great narrative, minor narrative,

accompanied by screams, moans, and a self-impressed climax of gibberish.

Children give names to the stars, mountain peaks, and rivers without climaxing,

and the middle-aged love nature, and to frolic in nature,

becoming one with the people, and not becoming one with the people, while
forgetting that you too are one of the people.

A bookstore owner with a high school education grabbed my arm all of a
sudden and said:

"I know you, you're an idealist!"

An idealist soars, dives, sits staring into space under a tree, watches the rain,

talks to the dead, blocks out the voices of all the living,

draws the curtains, builds a black box, constructs a universe,

and then thinks of Li Bai drawing his sword and looking around, at a loss.

The magpie wrote a book and the crow wrote a book.

The magpie doesn't understand the crow's language so asked the sparrow to
translate.

As long as there's speech there will be translation. How convenient to be deaf!

The frog makes noise in twenty different dialects. When animals curse each
other do they use bad words?

As long as there's love there will be cursing and bad words. Places of no cursing
or bad words are places of no love.

但好事者总是告诫我"不要以偏概全"。我记下了。

但我要用腹语向老天爷做思想汇报。从前在单位的汇报全属编造。

只要说方言，生活就有了温度。不过28度的生活通常听不懂42度的生活。

只要悲哀就能体验高尚，只要高尚就不长尾巴。

猴子们并不以高尚为尺度选出猴王。

霸道者从不梦想谦卑者能得到的好处。霸道者的想象力衰退。

说话也得有王法。哪一句振振有词的话里没有私心？

———————————————————

上海滩的黑道大哥把他的书法写出了天价。这没什么。

听听郁达夫的疯话：他说陆小曼是20世纪中国的普罗米修斯。

而大胡子马克思说："我才是普罗米修斯"。

受得了马克思但受不了郁达夫和陆小曼。

跟陆小曼八竿子打不着的郁达夫赞美这可人儿仿佛管闲事。

其丈夫徐志摩和情友胡适之都没这么说过。

But busybodies always warn me, "Don't make sweeping generalizations." I make a note of it.

But I use ventriloquism to report my thoughts to heaven. All my reports at work were fabrications.

As long as you're speaking dialect, life has warmth. But life at 28° can't understand life at 42°.

As long as you're morose you can experience nobility, and as long as you're noble you won't grow a tail.

Monkeys don't choose their monkey king according to standards of nobility.

Tyrants never dream of the benefits the humble can reap. The imagination of tyrants is in decline.

To speak there must be law. Which sentence in a forceful speech is devoid of selfishness?

A gangster on the Shanghai Bund sells his calligraphy at astronomical prices. That's nothing.

Listen to Yu Dafu's crazy talk: He called Lu Xiaoman the Prometheus of twentieth-century China.

And Marx and his beard said: "I am Prometheus."

I can stand Marx but I can't stand Yu Dafu and Lu Xiaoman.

Yu Dafu didn't have anything to do with Lu Xiaoman in the slightest praising her is like sticking his nose where it doesn't belong.

Her husband Xu Zhimo and her friend and lover Hu Shi never said anything like that.

另外，圈子里的美人啊，也让人受不了。

普通人笨嘴拙舌过小日子只能重复美人的歌唱"你是人间四月天"，

可"四月是最残忍的季节"，美人的字正腔圆遇上艾略特的字正腔圆。

太多的胡扯，把我们镇住了。三分钟不知道说什么好。

只好赞美晚清的自由和民国的民主以及袁世凯的高风亮节。

好像有根有据的胡扯总是不可一世。我们被震住了。

————————————————————

胡扯，胡扯，然后吃上自己的胡扯，是勇敢，是境界。

真理，以病句的形式被说出，把我们镇住了。

空白，仿佛只有桥墩没有桥体的桥梁，把我们镇住了。

表述清晰的神经病把我们镇住了。

修辞学丢了它坐满秃顶老头的元老院。

"我没什么好说的"把我们镇住了。

把话说死的人，把我们镇住了。他的目的达到。新的目的产生。

一个人代表昆虫说话，另一个人代表神说话，把代表人说话的人废掉了

当亿万富翁代表草根说话时他就是要当总统。

Anyway, I can't stand her just for being that group's designated beautiful woman.

Average people slow in speech can only repeat that beautiful woman's line,
    "You're an April day in the human world,"

but "April is the cruellest month," the rotund articulation of the beautiful woman
    encountering the rotund articulation of T. S. Eliot.

All this shit, it's overpowering. Three minutes and I still don't know what to say.

May as well praise the freedom of the late Qing and the democracy of the
    Republican era and the sterling integrity of Yuan Shikai.

Shit that comes with the slightest bit of backing is always so arrogant. We're shocked.

———————————————

Shit, more shit, then eating your own shit, it's brave, it's sublime.

Truth uttered in asyntactic sentences is overpowering.

Empty spaces, like a bridge that's only archway and no structure, are overpowering.

Insanity that expresses clarity is overpowering.

Rhetoric loses its Roman senate of bald old men.

"I have nothing to say" is overpowering.

People who talk subjects to death are overpowering. They've met their goals.
    A new goal is born.

One person speaks for the insects, and another speaks for the gods, deposing
    the one who speaks for people

when a billionaire speaks for the grassroots of society he wants to be president.

特朗普做到了。知识分子不明白这是咋回事。

别高估了总统的德行。

草根也不愿意将世界交给蚂蚁。

要求合理的出现就是对现实的批判。

———————————————————

像罪犯一样工作，把自己创造为一个罪犯，能镇住谁？

我要吃肉。我要跳大神。我要彻夜歌唱,口吐白沫。

把鬼当成神，就像把魂当成灵魂。

神，好像召之即来，不信神的人是不相信神也要吃喝。

没有神就以鬼的名义说话，没有鬼就以国家的名义说话，

没有国家就以个人的名义说话。

莫桑比克的瓦金波用他那纯净的烟嗓唱出了非洲大草原的清晨，

这样个人的嗓音配得上民族解放的事业。

他想不通好朋友玛利亚怎么就做了妓女，走上邪道。想哭，就絮叨。

在乱世里求知，在常世里玩乐。哪儿哪儿都一样。

Trump did this. Intellectuals just couldn't figure it out.

Don't overestimate the virtue of being president.

Even the grassroots of society don't want to give the world to ants.

To demand the appearance of reason is to criticize reality.

To work like a criminal, to make yourself into a criminal, who will that
overpower?

I want to eat meat. I want to go on a vision quest. I want to sing all night long,
frothing at the mouth.

To turn ghosts into gods is like turning spirits into souls.

The gods come as soon as they're beckoned. Atheists don't believe the gods still
need to eat or drink.

When there are no gods speak in the name of ghosts, and when there are no
ghosts speak in the name of the nation,

and when there is no nation speak in the name of the individual.

Wazimbo of Mozambique sings the morning of the African savannah with his
pure, smoky voice,

making an individual voice worthy of a cause like national liberation.

He can't figure out how his friend Maria could have become a prostitute, could
stray from virtue's path. He wants to cry but blabbers.

Seek knowledge in a chaotic world, and play around in an ordinary world.
Wherever you are it's the same.

我开车听着瓦金波。我的城市我的人世间从窗外掠过。

我的城外，不进城的花朵按照她们自己的标准长成红颜。

———————————————————

孔夫子听不懂柏拉图倒不是因为语言的关系。

孟夫子不屑于子墨子正因为他们说同一种语言。

韩非子灭了所有文化人。灭韩非子的人没什么文化。

棋圣也有下臭棋的时候，书圣也有写错字的时候，

不相信圣人没有拉肚子的时候。文武圣人不拉肚子诗圣也会拉肚子。

修到阿罗汉果位的人还拉屎不拉屎？佛教大分裂是因为智慧不够用？

西方净土究竟盖不盖房子？谁来盖？谁出图纸？

菩萨不在旷野里走路吗？菩萨不在黑暗里行动吗？

狮子在月光下喝水不是为了抒情。

女人在黄昏孤独地跳舞是抒情，但令人难过。

远去的飞鸟，自由地忍受孤独和饥饿。迎着灯红酒绿的死亡飞翔。

地下八千公里，左撇子阎王爷，用左手画勾，用业余的右手写诗。

I listen to Wazimbo while driving. My city and my world fly by outside the window.

Outside my city, the flowers that don't enter the city become beautiful by their own standards.

Confucius can't understand Plato but that has nothing to do with language.

Mencius disdains Mozi precisely because they speak the same language.

Han Feizi exterminates everyone with an education. Those who exterminate Han Feizi are the uneducated.

The sage of chess makes the wrong move sometimes, the sage of writing writes down the wrong word sometimes,

so I don't believe sages never get diarrhea. Even if the sage of civil and military affairs doesn't get diarrhea the sage of poetry does.

Do people who have achieved nirvana still take a shit? Did the great Buddhist schism happen because there wasn't enough wisdom to go around?

Do they build houses in Pure Land Buddhism? Who would do the building? Who draws up the blueprints?

Do bodhisattvas not walk in the wilderness? Do bodhisattvas not move at night?

Lions drink water in the moonlight but not for the sake of lyricism.

A woman dancing alone at dusk is lyrical, though it makes you sad.

Bird in the distance, flying away, freely enduring its loneliness and hunger. Soaring into a red-light nightlife death.

Eight thousand km underground, the left-handed king of the underworld draws a hook with his left hand, but writes poetry with his amateur right hand.

莎士比亚不是左撇子，但从来不曾梦想过要成为莎士比亚。

莎士比亚怎敢端教授的饭碗，尤其中国教授的饭碗！

一哭二闹三上吊，谁不会？但不是人人都敢这么做。

教授们尤其不敢这么做。但端了他的饭碗就没准了。

当一个艺术家追求真理的时候他恬不知耻地变成了哲学家和政治家。

当他厌倦了追求真理而又要活得好的时候他变成了政客或者商人。

失败的艺术家和诗人们改造世界。

干得不错的艺术家和诗人们往往被改造。

大妈从圣经读出狗屁不通的心得然后在汽车站上抓住我要我相信。

大姐从佛经读出狗屁不通的心得然后在饭桌上朝我翻白眼。

大哥和小弟从海德格尔与福柯读出狗屁不通的心得然后写狗屁不通的诗句。

大叔照着《唐诗三百首》写诗照着《芥子园画传》画画没人敢怎么着他。

写楷书的喜欢骂写草书的。写繁体字的喜欢骂写简体字的。

Shakespeare wasn't left-handed, but he never dreamed of becoming Shakespeare.

How could Shakespeare dare steal a professor's job, especially a professor in China?

Cry and fuss and raise a ruckus—who can't do that? But not everyone dares to act like that.

A professor most of all is unwilling to act like that. But if someone was stealing their job, then maybe.

When an artist is in pursuit of the truth he shamelessly becomes a philosopher and statesman.

When he's tired of pursuing the truth and wants to go back to living a good life he's a politician or a businessman.

Failed artists and poets change the world.

Artists and poets who do well usually end up reformed.

This old lady read the Bible and made a bunch of bullshit observations and then grabbed me at the bus stop needing me to believe.

Another woman read Buddhist scriptures and made a bunch of bullshit observations and then rolled her eyes at me at dinner.

Two brothers read Heidegger and Foucault and made a bunch of bullshit observations and then wrote a bunch of bullshit poems.

Uncle wrote poems based on *Three Hundred Tang Poems* and painted paintings based on *The Manual of the Mustard Seed Garden* and nobody dared say anything.

People who write calligraphy in *kai style* like to berate those who write in *grass style*. People who write traditional characters like to berate those who write simplified characters.

都是可怜人。可怜人的良苦用心救不了世界。

可怜人变成网络喷子和杠精。运交华盖的土鳖能让钱憋死。

历经磨难、大梦醒来、若有所失的有钱人像嬉皮一样跟上仁波切。

───────────────────────

天才就是缺乏推理能力的人。

二流画家就是能把画画到完美而没有意义的人。

模棱两可的世界也刮风也下雨。

模棱两可的世界引发一声浩叹。

不光盐是严肃的，酱油也是严肃的。

酱油和石油都是油吗? 有人为石油而战，有人为酱油而战。

麦子变成面包的历史不是麦子变成馒头的历史

饥饿的问题解决了，开始解决吃相的问题。

过去时代的吃相成了少数人怀旧的内容。

没有吃相的人像露水一样蒸发了。

───────────────────────

Pitiable, all of them. The world will not be saved by the good intentions of the pitiable.

The pitiable turn into internet trolls. Ground beetles born under a bad sign can suffocate even money.

After experiencing hardships and waking from an epic dream, the rich man who feels a sense of emptiness keeps up with the Rinpoches like a hippie.

———————————————

A genius is someone who lacks deductive reasoning.

Second-rate painters are those who can paint with perfection but no meaning.

In an ambiguous world the wind blows and it rains.

An ambiguous world gives rise to a deep sigh.

Not just salt is serious, sesame oil is serious, too.

Are sesame oil and petroleum oil both oils? Some fight over petroleum and some fight over sesame oil.

The history of wheat turning into bread is not the history of wheat turning into steamed buns;

after the problem of hunger is solved, there's still the problem of table manners.

The table manners of the past are a point of nostalgia for the few.

People with no table manners evaporate like the dew.

———————————————

当代的中古，换个说法：当代的中世纪。穿古装的小姐姐们可爱到爆炸。

改头换面的中世纪。改头换面的麻木。宅男们上网穿越到旧时代的新世界。

戴口罩的小奶狗。麻木的狂欢，无止境，直到死，直到撞上休止符。

作曲家都是坏人。他们知道怎样使用休止符，

就像黑道大哥、魔鬼和阎王爷知道怎样使用 死。

男人不作为男人，女人不作为女人。不是退步，只能是进步。

成人像小孩子一样撒娇，不作为成人。呀呀好有趣。

践踏花草的人，在墙角里傻笑。听见花草的抱怨，用娘娘腔。

践踏花草的人被管闲事的人举报。

小学教师有资格教训小学生，居委会大妈有资格教训所有人。

————————————————————

自豪于小农经济思维的新时代居委会的缺心眼儿的审美和不害臊。

封建主义宗法社会大农村的安静的害羞和嗷嗷叫的野蛮。

The contemporary medieval, or to put it differently: the contemporary middle
   ages. The young ladies dressed up in period dress are so adorable they're
   about to explode.

The shapeshifting middle ages. Shapeshifting numbness. At home online the otaku
   travel to a new world of an earlier era.

A little whelp in a facemask. Numb ecstasy, not stopping—until death, until it
   hits a rest.

Composers are bad people. They know how to use rests,

like gangsters and demons and the king of the underworld know how to use death.

Men don't act like men, and women don't act like women. It's not regression, it
   can only be progress.

Grownups who act like spoiled children aren't like grownups. Ah, what fun.

The people who trampled on the flowers are smirking in the corner. They heard
   the flowers complaining, sounding like pansies.

The people who trampled on the flowers were reported on by someone sticking
   his nose where it doesn't belong.

The grammar school instructor is qualified to lecture grammar school students,
   but the old ladies from the neighborhood committee are qualified to
   lecture everyone.

The dimwitted aesthetic and lack of shame of a neighborhood committee
   taking pride in a new era of small-scale peasantry economic thought.

The quiet shyness and squealing savagery of a large rural feudalist patriarchal society.

资本主义大城市大公司里理性到反人性的野蛮和人道主义高调的害羞。

罗马帝国的君主们所不理解的帝国主义文明等级论的不讲理和好意思。

把事情弄砸。啊，就这么干。人性好一会儿坏一会儿。就这么干。

阿育王信佛是为了杀掉耆那教徒和邪命教徒。

希特勒吃素当奥斯维辛的天空发臭。

吃人的塞拉西皇帝为民族独立而奋斗，腋下夹着黄金权杖。

军阀吴佩孚，晚年清心，书法有成就。

打嗝放屁背唐诗。啊，就这么干。

我温情脉脉，又滚滚向前。就这么干。

我笨拙的学习一直在持续。让我荒唐一下，让我荒凉一下

每一朵云我都是第一次看到。

啊，精彩！

————————————————————

失败而批判。或者为了批判而假装失败。干得好！

堕落而拒绝下地狱。堕落而获得活下去的理由。干得好！

这尘世：看风景的人关心自我，看街道的人关心他人。

The rationalism to the point of inhuman savagery and humanist high-strung shyness of capitalist urban corporations.

The unreasonableness and nerve of the hierarchical imperialist civilization the Roman emperors wouldn't understand.

Want to mess things up? Yeah, that's the way to do it. Human nature is good for a bit, then bad. That's the way to do it.

Ashoka became Buddhist to kill Jains and evil spirits.

Hitler was a vegetarian while the sky over Auschwitz reeked.

Man-eating emperor Haile Selassie fought for national liberation, a golden scepter under his arm.

Late in life, the warlord Wu Peifu cleared his mind and became an accomplished calligrapher.

Burp and fart and recite Tang poetry. Yeah, that's the way to do it.

I am full of tenderness. That's how I roll.

My clumsy studies continue. Let me be preposterous, let me be bleak

so every cloud is the first one I see.

Ah, glorious!

Fail and critique. Or to critique pretend to fail. Well done!

Fall but refuse to go to hell. Fall but gain a reason for living. Well done!

This world of dust: people who stare at landscapes care about themselves, while people who stare at the street care about others.

一个人把自己叫嚷成一群人。

一群人用一个声音说话就像一个人。

一个人走入人群但并未走入集体。

一个大集体地狱里也容不下天堂里也容不下，只好在大地上繁荣昌盛。

而天堂里也许有更高级的常世。

在知春路上，我看到天堂大厦的最底层开着一家麦当劳，

卖包子、饺子和炸鸡翅。

2018.7.5–2019.12.28

An individual shouts herself into a crowd.

A crowd speaks in one voice, like an individual.

An individual walks into a crowd but not into a collective.

A grand collective can't fit in hell and can't fit in heaven, so it's going to have to prosper on earth.

But heaven might have a higher ordinary world.

On Zhichun Road, I see that on the ground floor of Heaven Tower there's a McDonald's.

It sells steamed buns, dumplings, and fried chicken wings.

July 5, 2018 – December 28, 2019

悼念之问题

一只蚂蚁死去，无人悼念
一只鸟死去，无人悼念除非是朱鹮
一只猴子死去，猴子们悼念它
一只猴子死去，天灵盖被人撬开
一条鲨鱼死去，另一条鲨鱼继续奔游
一只老虎死去，有人悼念是悼念自己
一个人死去，有人悼念有人不悼念
一个人死去，有人悼念有人甚至鼓掌
一代人死去，下一代基本不悼念
一个国家死去，常常只留下轶事
连轶事都不留下的定非真正的国家
若非真正的国家，它死去无人悼念
无人悼念，风就白白地刮
河就白白地流，白白地冲刷岩石
白白地运动波光，白白地制造浪沫
河死去，轮不到人来悼念
风死去，轮不到人来悼念
河与风相伴到大海，大海广阔如庄子
广阔的大海死去，你也得死
龙王爷死去，你也得死
月亮不悼念，月亮上无人
星星不悼念，星星不是血肉

2014.11.11

Mourning Problems

an ant dies, and no one mourns
a bird dies, and no one mourns if it isn't a crested ibis
a monkey dies, and monkeys mourn
a monkey dies, and people pry open its skull
a shark dies, and another shark keeps swimming
a tiger dies, and some people mourning are mourning themselves
a person dies, and some people mourn and some people don't
a person dies, and some people mourn and some even applaud
a generation dies, and the next generation doesn't really mourn
a country dies, most of the time just leaving apocrypha
a country that doesn't leave apocrypha wasn't a real country
if it wasn't a real country, when it dies no one mourns
no one mourns, and the wind blows in vain
rivers flow in vain, washing over rocks in vain
glistening in vain, making vain ripples
the river dies, and it's not for man to mourn
the wind dies, and it's not for man to mourn
the river and wind make their way to the sea together, the sea as vast as
  Zhuangzi's sea
the vast sea dies, and you will have to die
the dragon king dies, and you will have to die
the moon doesn't mourn, there's no one on the moon
the stars don't mourn, the stars aren't flesh and blood

November 11, 2014

内部

一块石头的内部还是石头以及对地壳运动的记忆
一块砖的内部还是砖以及对火的记忆或者遗忘

一朵花，开放的花，没有内部，就像雨，没有内部
而一粒种子的内部是四季，是生长的欲望

一只苍蝇的内部是我不认识的血肉
一只鸡的内部是脏器、血管、肉和骨头以及对灵魂的呆滞

一个人的内部或者是一只老鼠或者是一条龙
一个人的内部或者是一座村庄或者是一泡尿一坨屎

一个人的内部肯定是黑暗的，没有星光
一个人的梦想渐渐消失在他的内部

一群人的内部还是人，一群人的内部还有高山和峡谷
一群人的内部，过去没有，但现在有了，是一座银行

一座银行的内部坐着一个行长，有时他也变成
一个囚犯，一个教师，一个演员，一个司令

但一个细胞的内部是一个宇宙，它并不起源于爆炸
但一个病毒的内部是咯咯笑的魔鬼

就像一场人间灾难的内部是心机，是误判，是愚蠢
或者一口气的内部是惊慌，是悲伤，是死亡

2020.5.10

Inside

inside stone is stone and the memory of plate tectonics
inside brick is brick and the memory or forgetting of fire

flower the blooming flower has no inside just as in rain there is no inside
but inside seed are the four seasons, the desire for growth

inside the fly is flesh and blood I do not know
inside the chicken are organs blood vessels flesh and bones plus a dullness of the
    spirit

inside each human is either a mouse or a dragon
inside each human is either a village or else a pool of piss and a pile of shit

inside each human is darkness, obviously—there's no starlight
everybody's dreams gradually disappear inside them

inside a group of people there are people and inside a group of people are
    mountains and valleys
inside a group of people there didn't used to be but now there is a bank

inside the bank is a branch president who sometimes ends up
a prisoner a teacher an actor a commander

but inside the cell is a universe that did not originate in an explosion
while inside the virus is a cackling demon

just as inside human disaster is scheming is misjudgment is foolishness
or inside breath is panic is sorrow is death

May 10, 2020

This Era Should Not Be Wasted:
Xi Chuan in conversation with Xu Zhiyuan

Xu Zhiyuan is a renowned author and media personality, and the host and producer of the influential online interview series Thirteen Invitations. *After going live in November of 2017, clips of his conversation with Xi Chuan gained over seventy million views. What follows is a translated transcript of this conversation edited for print.*

Xi Chuan meets Xu Zhiyuan at Seventh Prince's Grave (*Qiwangfen*) in the Western Hills outside Beijing, as he hopes to show Xu some of the ancient architecture around the site. Xi Chuan leads Xu up the deserted hill, only to find the path obstructed by a pile of scrap iron. They make their way over the obstruction but are blocked again by construction workers. They find a way around but the road comes to an end, so they start to head back.

Resting on the side of the road, Xi Chuan realizes the symbolism of the moment, as in Kafka's novel, where K. makes his way toward the Castle but can never reach it.

The dialogue between Xi Chuan and Xu Zhiyuan takes place in the courtyard of an inn they happen upon on their return.

Write out all that pressure to burden the page with it.

XI CHUAN: I talk about the early 1990s in one of my essays. For a long time, I would always find myself feeling awkward. I was always distracted, never knowing what I was doing or what I should be doing. Because in the '80s you had this feeling of, *I'm a poet.* But then in the '90s, you started to wonder if you or your writing meant anything. You feel powerless in that kind of environment: all the understanding you had built up about the world, about society, about literature and beauty, it all became invalid. All of a sudden you realize you're an idiot. So what are you going to do? But this is how we make it through the mess of life, even if it means we might piss our pants in the process.

XU ZHIYUAN: Were there any specific tactics you developed, to handle it all?

XC: No, I wrote, but I wasn't able to get much done. So I read as much as I could, book after book. I never let myself stop, never let myself be idle, so the books would overtake me. I never let myself face anything other than what was in books. That's how I was in those years.

XZ: How long did that last?

XC: I can't remember, because I did end up writing some things—which means taking all that pressure and transferring it into something else. If there's something you can't get past then write it out, burden the page with it, like you're unloading yourself. But this was a process that lasted a few years. I'm not sure when it ended.

XZ: In the '80s your poetry had a delicateness to it, and you adhered to certain poetic conventions. But then you began breaking these conventions in the '90s.

XC: It was the atmosphere of a new era.

XZ: When were you able to grasp that atmosphere with greater sensitivity? The atmosphere of the nineties was already very different from that of the eighties.

XC: It was the same atmosphere at the beginning of the '90s. It wasn't until Deng Xiaoping's "Southern Tour" of 1992, when he proclaimed that "to get rich is glorious," that things began to change. Then in about '97 or '98 we started to notice some people making a lot of money, and consuming, and the elements of entertainment starting to take over. At about that time a debate occurred, starting at a conference for poets and critics at the Panfeng Hotel, outside Beijing. Eventually this debate became known as the Panfeng Polemic. It sounds like something out of a martial arts novel: masters duking it out in a mountaintop inn, but in fact it was a conference at a hotel.

A few people, calling themselves "poets of the people," said that what writers like me—perhaps not just me—were doing was "Intellectual writing." The fact of the matter is that as much as I like intellectuals, I think of myself as an artist— that while I write poems with words, I think of myself instead as an artist whose medium happens to be language. There are many kinds of poets: some grow in the wild, and some read a lot of books. I've read a lot of books, but in the end I consider myself to be an artist, maybe because I spent so long teaching at an art school. The way I look at the world is the way artists look at the world. But at any rate, I ended up in the Intellectual camp.

The word "intellectual" in China was redefined in the 1980s. Why are there intellectuals? Just the other day I heard Dai Jinhua of Peking University criticizing the term. But there's a historical dimension to how it has been reused, which is that in the '80s, our age of Enlightenment, a group of people in Beijing put out a journal called *The Intellectual*. So it's a word that came into use in the '80s. At the time, in the literary world, to refer to art that wasn't "of the people," people would use the term "aristocratic"—they'd say for instance that you were too much of an aristocrat. But the problem was, there just weren't any aristocrats in China. So a new term was needed, to be more precise in defining those people who'd read a few books, who pondered issues, and who cared about the fate of the nation, which is how the word "intellectual" came about. Well, now the whole world is questioning the term, but the way I see it is that it comes out of a particular historical condition in China, so like it or not, "intellectual" is still going to pop up.

But back to the Panfeng Hotel. At the beginning of this debate I noticed something, which was that in this world, some people are going to be discussing things from an intellectual standpoint, and others will be taking a physical point of view, or the point of view of the day-to-day. Which is to say that our world is very rich, is just full of richness. Though my own writing isn't "of the people," I become aware of the quotidian through information gained via other channels. In one of my essays I mention a South African poet who asked me, "What do you know about South Africa?" I mentioned Nelson Mandela, apartheid. . . . And she asked, "What else?" I had to tell her I didn't know. What she meant was: Don't we have the day-to-day in South Africa, too? All you know are just signifiers. And I realized, yeah, my awareness of the quotidian didn't come from that debate but from other places.

xz: Just to interject—your mention of Mandela made me think of this: When I was in second or third grade, about 1986 or '87, so seven or eight years old, when the events in South Africa and Korea were all over the news each day, I wrote a poem. I wrote of what I imagined a victim of apartheid, a child about my age, must be going through, unable to go to the theater, unable to get a seat on a bus next to a white person, looking at a city in total loneliness. I don't know where the idea came from, and it's the only poem I ever wrote, and it certainly doesn't use any metaphor, or rhyme. . . . But I proudly showed it to my aunt, and she said, "How can you call this a poem? It doesn't rhyme!" And I never wrote another poem. I must have had a poet's dream deferred!

xc: I was reprimanded, too: *Why don't you write fiction?* Well, because one time I wrote a story and sent it in to a magazine, and the editor wrote back and said, "Maybe you should send us some poems."

xz: When was this?

xc: I don't remember the year, but it extinguished any residual interest I had in writing fiction. But let me ask you: When you wrote that poem, did you really imagine yourself as Black?

xz: I'm not sure, it was just the intuitive writing of a child.

xc: Yeah, that's very interesting. Why did I ask that? I think when we care about something, what we really care about may just be a part of it. Apartheid, for instance. We may empathize, but we aren't quite imagining ourselves as Black. When we accept an idea, we don't necessarily know what its context is. When did you have your first impulse to write? When you first became aware of it? For me, I initially wanted to be a painter, not a poet. In high school I wrote some classical-style poems—not real classical poems, just copies of those "there's a poem as proof" pieces from *Outlaws of the Marsh*. But at university, I got pulled in: everyone was writing poetry—modern poetry.

xz: What were your impressions of Peking University? Did you have a sense of superiority when you started?

xc: There was no sense of superiority. One impression I had when I started at PKU was, "This campus is very pretty!" But another concerned the library: all these things I'd never read before, which I could now find, right in the library. We were still basking in the glow of the end of the Cultural Revolution then. The first two books I read at PKU were the Bible—because I had heard of it but had never come across a copy (there it was in the open stacks, a reprint of the Bible: thick, heavy, a banned book)—and *Family* by Ba Jin. So I read the Bible and I read Ba Jin's *Family*! The second one I'm not sure why. It must have been another book I had heard about but hadn't come across before. Why was the library so important? Because it was a place where you could learn on your own. I remember we used to say that even though we were supposed to be studying at PKU, the real learning we did was outside our individual classes. That's a bit overstated, of course—there were a lot of great teachers there. And learning on our own simply involved finding books in the library and reading like crazy. This is a habit I've kept, and probably you have, too. You have to read every day, no matter how exhausted you might feel. You've got to read at minumum a few pages. I spend at least an hour reading every day.

Modernism helps us break out of the shell of the past, to become modern.

XZ: I know you probably don't want to talk too much about Haizi and Luo Yihe, but I see that you have recently edited a collection of their poetry, and included a written remembrance for each of them, about how you met.

XC: I wrote those not long after they had died, so those pieces are full of pathos.

XZ: You were young men, in your early twenties.

XC: We were in our early twenties. Of the three of us, Luo Yihe was the oldest, and had read the most—more than anyone majoring in Chinese—and had seen a lot. He'd spent time as a peasant with his parents during the Cultural Revolution when they were sent down to the country. His poems "walked the right road beneath heaven," with the quality of what Mencius calls "the grand." Even though he never really talked about the problems of tradition, his conduct adhered to China's Confucian tradition. At that point, Haizi and I hadn't published anything yet, but Luo Yihe's name was already appearing in journals. Someone like that, with such a wealth of experience, it was always compelling how he looked at things, compelling just to talk to him. Sometimes when you chat with someone like that you feel like you can't get enough.

XZ: More compelling than talking with you?

XC: I'm nothing compared to him. And Haizi I got to know later, in his last year at PKU in 1983. I could tell even then that his poetry was different, but I didn't really understand his true talent until later on. I wrote a letter to someone to introduce this friend of mine, saying he was going to be very distinguished one day. That was when I became willing to use the word "genius" to describe him.

XZ: Is it liberating to meet a genius roughly the same age as you, or does it create oppression and anxiety?

XC: You'll feel oppressed and anxious if you're vain and jealous that they're better known. If you're not vain or competitive, there's no oppression—they're your friends. In those days we were all putting out mimeographed books and journals, and one time Haizi and I were talking and one of us said, Let's you and me put out a book together! So we did, under the title *Urn of the Wheatfield*. Why on earth did we give it such a bizarre title! Maybe we were thinking of Wallace Stevens's "Anecdote of the Jar"?

XZ: Youth is a good time for these kinds of provocations.

XC: Youth is a very good time for these provocations. Not just Haizi, but the whole slew of poets in Beijing at the time, we'd have a reading in someone's apartment—in those days we didn't call them readings, we called them "plays": a bunch of us would sit in a room, bottles in hand (I can't drink, but they'd be drinking), and shout, "Play another one! Play another one!" and someone would stand up and play a poem. That was the atmosphere of our "playing."

XZ: What would happen when you'd play a poem?

XC: I used to play. Heh. Beijing in those days was split into all sorts of camps: a camp in the schools, then in the so-called real world a few other camps, including the Old Summer Palace Poetry Society, the Daxian poetry camp, the Hei Dachun followers, the Xue Di society, whose president was Dai Jie—no one even knows where Dai Jie is anymore! When I'd go visit them it was like walking into an underground organization. In the inner room there'd be some secret business transaction going down—selling asphalt or something, since they were always looking for ways to make money—and in the outer room they'd be talking poetry. The table was lit up by a lightbulb they pulled down from the roof, pulled so low it almost touched the tabletop. Dai Jie opened up a drawer, whipped out a wad of bills, slapped it on the table, and said, "See that, Xi Chuan? That's our budget for putting on these plays!" There was one guy who was always getting into fights, a hooligan but who wrote poetry, loved poetry. He said to me, "Xi Chuan, if anyone tries to give you trouble, just call me!" I felt like someone had my back!

XZ: Your camp must have all been born in the '60s. Did you have any sort of impulse for rebellion? Like for instance the Manghan poets in Chengdu, Sichuan: what they rebelled against was pretty obvious. Was it as obvious with your group?

XC: Discontent, rebellion—these are features of youth everywhere. But Chengdu isn't Beijing. The young poets there were working against the Obscure poets of Beijing. But in Beijing we younger poets and the Obscure poets, we all knew each other. We were not antagonistic. The word with the Old Summer Palace poets was *pass* (like, *pass* as in playing cards). Then one time at the Beijing YMCA one of the guys said to Bei Dao, "We're going to *pass* you." He meant it as a joke, and everyone there took it as a joke, but when people who weren't there heard about it, it got written as literary history, and then turned into an attitude, and people didn't find it funny anymore. They took it as a serious issue. So in literary history, or in fact in history of any kind, there are bound to be misunderstandings. Some of the words we use come out of specific moments, with their own moods, but when those words are repeated without the original context, misunderstandings are to be expected.

XZ: What were your tastes in literature, in poetry, in those days?

XC: For me—and not just for me, in fact—something important about the time was the need to get up to date in our study of literary history, an important part of which meant reading modernism from the west, including Russia and Latin America. What we had been reading up to that point was all revolutionary romanticism and realism, all that business coming from the Soviet Union, from Gorky. Reading modernism made us feel like we were breaking out of the shell of the past, becoming modern, becoming like the people in other countries—a process of self-modernization.

It was a very interesting process. I remember talking about it with an American poet, saying that though we've read the same things as they read in America, the results were all very different. Why? Because literary history in the west is wave upon wave: there's romanticism, then after that there's modernism, and after that there's postmodernism. But we just read it all at once, jumbled together. And what happened? We read works of modernism, but might understand it in terms of romanticism; when I read works of postmodernism, maybe I can't tell the difference between that and modernism. Not that I'm interested in these concepts anymore, anyway. All the -isms of the past seem to me to have been devised for second-rate figures of limited creativity, who have to adhere to some principle or other, some -ism, so that they have a direction to go in. The people who are really strong and creative will pass those -isms by. But you have a period in life where you do need to understand those movements. I spent my time doing that after the Cultural Revolution, when I read everything I could, a bit like Rabelais's Gargantua. So if we understand literature a little differently, well, that was caused by history, too.

XZ: In the latter half of the 1980s, when you started writing poetry, that's when the taste for modernism was strongest.

XC: I started writing poetry in the early '80s. But you're right, at the time I was following a lot of European and American modernism, even though before that I had always been interested in the Chinese traditions. Then my thinking was liberated, and most of what I was reading was European and American literature, like Yeats, Eliot, Pound, Valéry, Rilke, Baudelaire. . . .

XZ: When I got to PKU in 1995, the modernists were still on top. Yeats was the greatest at the time, it seemed.

XC: Yes. "When you are old and grey and full of sleep, / And nodding by the fire, take down this book, / And slowly read, and dream of the soft look / Your eyes had once, and of their shadows deep; // How many loved your moments of glad grace, / And loved your beauty with love false or true, / But one man loved the pilgrim soul in you, / And loved the sorrows of your changing face . . ." I can't remember more than that. Poems like this are wonderful. Or the Russian poet Anna Akhmatova: "I bend over them as if over a cup" [Judith Hemschemeyer, trans.]—incredible. If you've never come across such poems then you'd never know what you have missed but once you do the way it affects you . . . it's not like a gentle breeze or light rain, it's like a great tsunami crashing over you! I don't write like that anymore, but I have no regrets whatsoever for having read them, as it's the process through which I became modern. Another line that's just amazing is from Rimbaud, talking about a cow, grazing—for us in China a cow would be like an old peasant facing down to the yellow earth, back under the sun—but for Rimbaud, it's "the peaceful beasts that graze down to the sea of Palestine" [Louise Varèse, trans.]! What kind of thinking could produce this? You know what it means to be shocked? Just *that*—wow!

XZ: There were a lot of poets in the '80s. The lines that made it into broader society and which resonated through the era were all in the high lyric mode. But you weren't writing this kind of work, or weren't trying to write these kinds of poems. Is that something you regret?

XC: That's not something I regret. I wasn't the only one writing. Four other classmates and I mimeographed a small collection on hand-cut wax paper titled *Five Colored Stones*. Of the five of us, I'm the only one still writing. One committed suicide and one became a translator; the two women stopped writing.

XZ: Or to put it differently: becoming an idol doesn't hold any attraction for you?

XC: Not at the time. If Yang Lian, for instance, came to campus to give a talk, you'd go listen! But it never occurred to me that one day I might become a Yang Lian. I heard Gu Cheng give a talk at Beijing Normal University and I never felt the urge to become someone like Gu Cheng. Actually, I didn't really like Gu Cheng's work, but I went to hear him anyway. Late Gu Cheng was much more interesting to me than early Gu Cheng; most people like early Gu Cheng, but it's a bit too sweet for me: "there's already a drop of sun / sweet and red / on the morning fence" [Joseph R. Allen, trans.]—so saccharine! But he was famous, people liked it.

xz: In your memorial of Luo Yihe and Haizi, you wrote that their departure represents the loss of a whole dimension of literature.

xc: Luo Yihe always emphasized literary health. There are a lot of illnesses in literature, a lot of unhealthy things. We had a classmate who would take a run around the university track, then come back and write a poem. We all said he'd never make it, getting all worked up from running and then trying to write poetry. In the end he did stop writing. Luo Yihe wasn't talking about health physiologically, of course, but he did have a kind of a standard of health. This was one dimension. Twentieth-century western literature—as well as regional literature heavily influenced by western literature—is full of unhealthiness, of disease, of groaning. Of course what you'll find is that it's exceptionally difficult to write healthy literature. We don't know how to write positive, healthy characters.

xz: The whole of literary history is just a metaphor for disease.

xc: World literature in the twentieth century is full of it. Only in literature of the so-called Third World, where literature is a weapon in movements of national independence or national liberation, are you going to find a healthy sort of literature. Maybe that's a bit too extreme, but most literature has something to do with sickness, being unhealthy, sadness, suffering. . . . Of course this gets at a more complex issue: if literature can be boiled down to nothing but method then how can it encompass all the details of our lives. Without our elders the modernists we could only attempt to write like a blind man feeling his way. But then, I think it's only through trial and experiment that the possible exists, so maybe we'll end up writing something different. I didn't understand this when I was younger, hadn't realized then how modernism means different things in China and in the west, with their different environments and different audiences.

Later I wrote an essay on the modernism of Mu Dan: his was an incomplete modernism. He started out as a writer in the chaos of war, which shaped his writing into a kind of "shrunken modernism," diminishing it. I've also written about how in China we love to talk about uniting east and west, but, well, how can you really do that? One result from uniting east and west might be the culture of Japan. Some Chinese artists and poets try to unite east and west and fail. So what do they do? They end up diminishing both cultures, diminishing both east and west! Maybe you can unite a diminished east with a diminished west, but it's hard to put a strong western mindset and a strong ancient Chinese mindset together. For instance, no one has tried to unite Dante with Sima Xiangru. It can't be done!

XZ: So what do you do?

XC: Well I do want to see Dante and Sima Xiangru all tangled up with one another, damn it! That's where I might try to be more forceful than some other Chinese poets.

The era I'm most infatuated with is the Warring States, since my true dream is to be near the masters.

XZ: In 1992 you started teaching at the Central Academy of Fine Arts. Was that a big change for you?

XC: Yes.

XZ: Do you think that if you had stayed at PKU, or had stayed within a circle of writers, your writing would have ended up differently?

XC: I graduated from PKU, but before going to CAFA I was working as an editor at a magazine published by Xinhua. I started teaching in '92, but the writers I was friends with then haven't changed.

XZ: What kind of perspective did CAFA give you?

XC: Its impact on me accumulated over many years. I've always had a passion for the visual arts and enjoy hanging out with artists; I felt most at ease in that crowd. That's why I went to work at CAFA. The changes didn't permeate my being all at once, but took a long time to take shape. When I was writing *Salute*, I felt a little broken, fragmented, since I had given up my earlier style of writing. As I couldn't write the same way, all I knew how to do was to write randomly, so I took up my old notes and compiled them into *Salute*. Only the central section, "Beast," was written start to finish, about a kind of ineffable monster coming toward me. In those days I felt like I was being overwhelmed by things I couldn't control, no matter what I did. Like it or not, such things appear and swarm all around you. . . . This kind of change in my writing wasn't something that happened on a whim.

My trip to India in 1997 also opened something up in me. Take the daily act of needing to piss! Here in China you have to look for a restroom. But while traveling in India, I observed that if there were no restrooms it was acceptable to just go on the street. I remember being stunned at how people could live like that. Such a different way of thinking about things in India! I was overcome with culture shock: *They can do that?* But as it kept on happening, it opened something up in me.

xz: Can you elaborate more? How did Indian ways of thinking open up your aesthetics?

xc: For instance, I got tricked one time. I visited a temple and saw two men sitting inside. They called me over and asked me to close my eyes, and one of them touched the center of my forehead with a finger dipped in red. I figured this meant that I had been blessed, and I felt very grateful. Then he waved a ten-rupee note in front of me, as if to say that's how much I owed him—it costs money to get a blessing! Ten rupees isn't much, so I gave it to him. But when I got back to my hotel and looked in the mirror, I found that there was no red dot on my forehead! He must have switched fingers when my eyes were closed—he didn't even want to part with that little bit of red! I was stumped. But that's life. Being tricked is part of life.

Or another time, I was buying a train ticket from Delhi to Agra. It should have been ₹900 but I didn't know this at the time and the salesperson behind the counter charged me ₹1900. Only after I was on the train, chatting with a young woman from England, did I learn that the ticket should have been ₹900. He had cheated me out of more than the cost of the ticket itself! But eventually I got used to the way things worked there, and the more I traveled the cheaper things got as I slowly figured out how not to get fooled. My time in India affected me pretty deeply, in the sense that I learned that things wouldn't always go the way you were used to, that other worlds were possible. I had previously thought of things in terms of China and the west, but then it became China—India—the west, a triangular perspective.

xz: How did this manifest itself in your writing?

xc: It was in India that I started writing *Eagle's Words*, and finished it after returning to Beijing. But putting that kind of perspective into my work felt strange, so for half a year after I completed the manuscript I didn't say anything about it to anybody. Had I written this? It seemed like the work of someone else, like something stolen. I had to keep it in the drawer for a while, spend half a year acclimating to it, before I could talk to anyone about it.

There's another book I should mention, *Genghis Khan and the Making of the Modern World* by Jack Weatherford. He talks about the Mongols on the steppe, how their cavalry didn't ride in formation, and they had no need for roads, but would attack like lightning, seemingly from every direction. It turns out Hitler's *blitzkrieg* was a tactic learned from the Mongols. Since there were no provisions to support these cavalry, the soldiers would have five horses, one to ride and the other four to be slaughtered as meat, their blood for drinking—totally different from how the Chinese armies would fight. Chinese armies would steal provisions during battle. In the end the lords of the Golden Horde assembled and said, "Well, we've conquered all this land—where next?" They couldn't make up their minds, so eventually the Mongols decided, "Hell, let's just attack in every direction!" They attacked Europe and they attacked China, which is how the Yuan dynasty was established. Reading this I thought to myself, "What *is* this?" But it was incredible! Nothing like the way I had been taught to think! How wonderful! There were only a hundred thousand Mongol horsemen, barely enough to fill a football stadium, but this small army (plus mercenaries and the soldiers of surrendered armies) could conquer the world. It's fascinating to consider. All of this was just such a provocation, such an inspiration, to my way of thinking and to my writing. Unbelievable!

XZ: You wish you could have a Mongolian kind of thinking and writing?

XC: No, no, what I wish for isn't a Mongolian kind of thinking or writing. What I really wish for is to have the kind of writing of the masters from the Warring States period [475–221 BCE]. These days everyone reads the poetry of the Tang and Song—and I read that, too—but the era I'm really infatuated with is the Warring States.

XZ: Why is that?

XC: Many reasons. For one, the writers had such talent. For another, the Warring States masters were really working through their own era. Some people want to pull time backward, like Confucius at the end of the Springs and Autumns period. And then there are those who don't look to the past, like the Legalists. After the Cultural Revolution and its replaying of the debates between Confucianists and Legalists, everyone likes to say that the Legalists were dictators—and dictatorship was a real thing in the Warring States era, too—but if you really read Han Fei, pushing aside all our current ways of looking at Legalism, you find that Han Fei was the kind of thinker who really looked intently at his times. He really achieved a depth, in addition to an astounding breadth.

xz: Do you think Han Fei was like our version of Thomas Hobbes?

xc: If you consider them in terms of their designs on the nation, sure, why not. Hobbes had his designs for England, and Han Fei his designs for China, to similar effect. But I really don't want to oversimplify the issue.

The *Huainanzi* talks about Yangzi shedding tears at a fork in the road and Mozi weeping over undyed silk. That is, Mozi saw undyed silk and didn't know if it was going to end up black or yellow, so he cried, and Yangzi came to a fork in the road and didn't know if it was going to take him north or south, so he cried, too. I find these two moments especially moving. I remember having a deep sense of identification with Warring States thought in the 1990s—are things going to go north or south? The intelligent people of the day were worrying over so many questions, with answers to none of them, and all they could do was cry. And not only Mozi and Yangzi, but Confucius was crying, too—he cried when he saw the mythical *qilin*, in year fourteen of the reign of Duke Ai of Lu [481 BCE], and gave up writing the *Springs and Autumns*. These three moments pointed me to where the heights of Chinese culture reside. Despite all the reading I've done in western culture, I know of the heights of Chinese culture and the writers' relationship with the fates of the people who have lived on this land back then. So the era I'm most passionate about, the era I yearn for, is the Warring States, which I would extend all the way to the Han [206 BCE–220 CE]. My true dream isn't to write Tang or Song poetry, it's to be near those masters.

xz: Whom do you feel closest to, among the masters?

xc: I like Zhuangzi. But they're all great. If I had to pick one book, I'd want all their works collected into a single volume!

It's the mud and sand of life in the era that give me nourishment.

xz: Has working through one's era always been the main enticement for you?

xc: Yes. If you're not working through your era, your language, then your understanding of literature will belong to someone else. In the US they say that artists avoid unoriginality like the plague. You can't be like other people. You can't be like Rilke, you can't be like Yeats, et cetera. So I've always said that no matter how much I love Borges, there's no point in being a second Borges. Artists need creativity. But where does this creativity come from? Weaker poets are going to write according to a received sense of literature, with the words and education of a received literary sensibility. But people with more of a pioneering spirit aren't like that. All my materials are raw. Working through these raw materials, I may be successful, I may fall on my face, but maybe something entirely unexpected could happen.

XZ: We'll call you the poet of raw meat.

XC: All right, I'll be the raw meat poet, even though I don't eat much meat! I've always cared about working through the life of one's own era. Most people will avoid things that don't fit their taste, but I've always tried not to avoid things. I figure that as a poet-artist I've got to learn how to get what I can even from things that aren't necessarily my taste.

I tend to think that we get inspiration where we expect it least, and I love to experience the mud and sand of living in an era. Last night I participated in an event where we discussed Roberto Bolaño. I said there's a grit to his poetry, mud and sand, along with majesty. His working method was one of vigorousness, dripping with vitality. I need nourishment. Anyone working needs nourishment. And I know that mud itself is among the things that give me nourishment. There's a patron of the arts in the UK—he says that 99% of contemporary art is trash, but his support is for the future of the one percent. I think that's a pretty interesting way of looking at it.

XZ: China in the 1990s was the China of the artists. Were they working through the era more sharply? From an outsider's perspective, in the '80s it was the poets who were working through the era most passionately, but in the '90s it was the visual artists.

XC: Yes and no. The reason you started noticing visual art was because they started making big money, and once it turned into money, it became something, became the object of media attention. Once it became something you started to feel that contemporary art was part of China's vitality. But because I'm as close as I am to so many artists, I have a good sense of their approach. First, contemporary art in China is an experimental art, and to put it bluntly it faces westward—largely because from painting to installation art, you're not going to find a buyer in Pakistan. So let's not have any romantic illusions when we talk about contemporary Chinese art: when they say "international" what they mean is the west.

XZ: And a very narrow view of the west, at that.

XC: The contemporary art market itself is western. The big auction houses, the big galleries, that's all western capital. They are driving tastes in contemporary art, setting its value. But collectors can be interesting when you look closely at them, too. A lot of collectors aren't Chinese bosses, and they're not from the west—neither Europe nor the US. They're ethnic Chinese from Southeast Asia. This is one of the secrets of the business of contemporary Chinese. But that's another topic.

Here, it's important to ask, "What are the resources China can use?" The western market allocates you a certain culture as your market share, encouraging you to produce art of a certain kind. As a Chinese artist you have the responsibility to make use of your tradition, and if you play it right, you can succeed. I met this funny artist in Germany who always wore a Manchu jacket, liked to meditate, and would spew mysticism whenever he spoke to westerners. My German friends said, "Hey, let's introduce you to the modern Confucius!" As soon as I laid eyes on him I knew I was dealing with a charlatan. He made oil paintings: he'd start with a Chinese-style landscape, then paint over it in white so the image would look very shadowy and vague, you know—somewhere between presence and absence. He had found a way to claim both Chinese tradition and the western contemporary aesthetic: landscape, the Dao, Zen, absence, minimalism.

xz: I'm curious about how one might work through this era. Were the nineties a time of general loss for poets?

xc: Actually, I think visual artists weren't able to enter the era very well, either. I heard an extreme statement, that in the nineties, after real estate, it was visual art that was the most profitable industry. They caught China's development at the right time: all these new buildings needed something to make them look good, so the wealthy started to buy art. The artists caught a good wave, and got very rich, but were they really working through the era? I don't think so.

xz: What does it take to respond to the era?

xc: Artists, writers, and poets will have all sorts of responses to an era. Some respond opportunistically, reacting right away to hot topics; others respond by straightening out the logic of history, work that takes much longer.

xz: And is much more arduous.

xc: For sure. You ask, "Why is our society the way it is right now?" If you trace history back—and why not start with Confucius?—it will take an immense amount of work.

xz: When did you start thinking about doing this kind of work, from a poet's point of view?

xc: Speaking as a poet, I feel the need to penetrate the historical logic of our society. Why? Poets today aren't as showy as we were in the '80s—for lots of reasons, one being that we're now living in a media society that chases event after event, event after event, with no discussion of historical logic and only manages to convey a kind of visual effect.

xz: Totally without memory.

xc: And with no historical memory—the whole environment, all of life, really, just runs along with youth culture: the most vibrant culture is youth culture, what makes money is youth culture, the celebrities are the celebrities of youth culture . . . our lifestyles are all about the wish to stay young, and the hosts of our TV shows are all young and attractive. And here's another interesting phenomenon: all rich people in contemporary China are *nouveau riche*, earning and spending new money, which carries its own lifestyle along with it.

xz: New money, new style.

xc: This isn't the kind of thing you can choose, either, since whatever point development reaches, that's the point where you're fixed. Take the speed of urbanization in China, for example. In the early '80s the urbanization rate was 13%. By the early '90s it was 26%. But now it's reached 57%. When we're all carrying new money in our wallets and spending new money, it doesn't take much to imagine what society's going to be like.

xz: How do you experience this complexity within media society? What about creativity?

xc: This is very complicated to talk about. For instance, in poetry—we say that poetry is for the young, that you rarely come across people in middle age who still write, and even fewer among the old. I'm not even talking about poets who publish in journals every so often, I'm talking about actual poets who can make discoveries in their poetry. I invited a number of foreign poets to China once, and I wanted to invite an equal number of Chinese poets to engage in dialogue with them. I had a very hard time because I couldn't find enough poets of both the equivalent age and intelligence! It was embarrassing. I call this situation in China "the post-1919 stress disorder"—though of course it's not limited to the

New Culture Movement of 1919. Guo Moruo's *Phoenix of Nirvana* was all about reform by the youth, the young becoming the hope of the world.

XZ: The worship of youth in the twentieth century.

XC: The worship of youth. In China, after the period of reform and liberation in the '80s, youth culture was a revolutionary youth culture. But as soon as it became wrapped up in the market it turned into consumer culture. The ideas of youth transform very quickly, faster than it takes to put up a building, and you can't keep up. A foreign poet once asked me, "Could China just slow down a little?" I said, I don't know! It might not be able to reduce its speed. It's not going to slow down just because you ask it to—it's already racing down the track of history. As Chinese people living in China, we understand this speed.

I used to live in a hutong off Mishi Street, in a place with a courtyard. The house had belonged to the Beijing opera actor Meng Xiaodong, and then was renovated into a compound with separate units. The residents didn't have their own bathroom—we all shared the one bathroom in the courtyard that didn't have any walls between the stalls. So when you were taking a shit you'd have a chat with the person taking a shit right next to you. By the time I had my own apartment, I would joke that I'd invite them all over to my place just so they could take a shit! I came to realize that courtyards might be beautiful but if they don't come with a private bathroom I'd rather live somewhere else, even if it means giving up the beauty of the courtyard, the common culture of the courtyard.

Once I heard a couple of foreigners complaining about the demolition of old Beijing. What they really wanted to see was a museum. But if Germany wants to sell cars to China, the roads need to be wide. If the roads are wide, however, the French won't be happy because they want to see a museum of old Beijing. So I joked with them, "You guys decide: do you want to sell us cars, or do you want us to be some kind of museum for you?" They laughed, forcefully. We live in China, we're in the field, and people in the field are faced with two kinds of morality: one is survival morality, and the other is cultural morality. Which one comes first? In this case, I'm going to put the former first, because I have parents, because I have siblings, so I want my own bathroom! Of course, cultural morality is also extremely important to me, but when there's a conflict between the two, I'm going to put survival morality first in order to *live* first—live with a little dignity. All this development bears a cost, a huge cost, but there's going to be a cost no matter what you do.

XZ: Do you mean that the birth of new phrases and youth culture can easily fall into a trap of cultural relativism? You could say that W. B. Yeats and Ezra Pound, or Hu Shi and Mu Dan, were creating new words, just as much as the youth of today are creating new words.

xc: Naturally, people have always invented new words, but when we say we're coining new words, we also need to be aware of how quickly things in this era become obsolete. I think of the word Milan Kundera popularized: *kitsch*. This word just sticks with us. In Chinese we've even developed an antonym for it.

xz: That's the life force of these new words.

xc: Yes, some words live a long time, and some are gone in an instant. Whoever knows pride—whether you're proud of your writing, or proud of your business, or proud of your political power—will always feel this shadow of a face right behind you called "obsolescence." The problem is that the proud never feel obsolescence standing behind them, and just keep on living blithely. But then there are other words that don't disappear once they have been created. These words are the true demonstration of historical logic.

Here's an inappropriate example: the Indian thinker Ashis Nandy wrote a paper about Coca-Cola. He says that in theory, we can all make our own beverages—plant an orange tree, squeeze orange juice—but Coca-Cola is something we cannot make. It's the product of a recipe. Nationalism in India is very strong, and not long after Coke entered the Indian market, they were squeezed out. Then Indians came up with their own brand of cola, Thums Up. Nandy said that Indians might have gotten rid of Coke, but even if you can't drink Coke, you can't get rid of the idea of Coke. Thums Up is just an imitative response to Coca-Cola. The coining of new words is like that: they're all inventions, but with different amounts of inventiveness. And you can't judge them in the moment. Of course, Coke itself later did return to India.

xz: The embarrassment you were talking about in the early '90s, when someone like you who was so devoted to the pursuit of artistic consciousness lived in a moment like that, did your anxiety produce more creativity or more exhaustion?

xc: The anxiety didn't affect me. Creativity has many faces. For instance, in creativity there's a tension—a lot of people use this word "tension"—such as the tension between someone's dream and reality. For some these are close, but for some they're more distant, and there's a historical element to this tension, too. In writing these are all possibilities. Not that I want to give anyone the impression that I'm completely out of tune with my era, since I'm not. People are bound to encounter things that have meaning, whether in their personal life, or in society . . . things that stimulate thought.

Speaking as a writer, I think we're living at a historical turning point, something I talk about in a book of essays called *A Bend in the Great River*. If I just wanted to preserve my existing state and not be open to new possibilities, I'd be wasting the era. And this era should not be wasted, any more than the '80s or the '90s should have been wasted. What would it mean for an era to be wasted? To ignore it, to live totally in your own head, to let this era pass you by. For an artist, you can't just write your own interiority, you have to have other materials for writing—and life itself is that material.

I have a Canadian poet friend who talks about how jealous he is of me. He says Canadian poets have nothing to write about—Canadians are all so nice. When they get off the bus, they say, "Thank you, have a nice day" to the driver! But I say to him, if I go back to China and say "Thank you, have a nice day" to the bus driver, people will think I'm insane—either that, or that I'm putting on airs. Or consider another example: when certain US poets have nothing else to write about, maybe they write about their fathers, or how they've come to know themselves through writing about their fathers. Of course, after they've written about their fathers they might write about Native Americans. All intellectuals with a conscience are full of shame about Native Americans, whom are often now called "First Peoples." Writing about this oppression at the hands of white people can be very powerful.

XZ: Some need another era to feel empathy with.

XC: Right, which we don't seem to need. Isn't the force of our reality strong enough already? All the jokes, all the absurdity, all the celebrity . . . as soon as you turn on your computer you're faced with the incomprehensibility of our society. From the point of view of literature, of writing, it's all very interesting. Here's something you think isn't worth spending the least amount of time or energy on, and everyone's just swarming toward it. But you only know who you are, only begin to know yourself, when you're not part of that swarm. Take the earthquake in Japan, the tsunami at Fukushima in 2011 that caused the nuclear reactor meltdown, and everyone became afraid of nuclear contamination spreading to China and so they rushed to the stores to buy salt. One guy bought five tons of salt! But who ever said that salt could protect you from nuclear fallout? What is the meaning of this rush? On the one hand it's fun: you get the thrill of participation. But behind the thrill there's something else: panic. Over time, of course, a society can cultivate fortitude. How can that be built up? Through the fortitude of culture.

Right now, many people feel like they don't want culture and feel the need to spit on culture. Only when you're panicked, and when you want to overcome that sense of panic, do you know that you need culture. Yet there's also something melodramatic and elitist about culture. I don't have to be elitist about it—popular culture is culture, too—but what do you know of popular culture if I don't talk to you about so-called elite culture? We don't need to talk about grandiose figures like Confucius; we can talk about Guandi temples: why are Yue Fei and Guan Yu worshipped together? There's a Double Guandi Temple in Beijing, in Xisi, in fact. Or what is the relationship between Daoism the religion and Daoism the philosophy? This is all culture, too, but no one understands it, so when you look online, all you get is either people praising you or bashing you. There's no fortitude, no fortitude for this kind of culture. Chinese culture has always possessed its Way. As Gu Yanwu wrote, in the seventeenth century, "If we bring back the language of the three Sage Kings, we bring back the Way of the three Sage Kings."

I can't write lyric poetry, because I've lost the ability to be purely lyrical.

xz: In the twentieth century China was full of marvels and absurdities that weren't successfully transformed into creativity, so a lot was wasted. But there's something more between absurdity and creativity, without which the absurd would never be able to inspire creativity.

xc: I published a speech once where I talked about the brevity of modernity and the lasting contemporary. As I see it, the problems of the twentieth century are still with us. I even think the problems of the late Qing, of the end of the nineteenth century, are still with us, undigested. I don't think the late Qing is gone; I don't think we've bid farewell to the revolution. The past isn't past.

xz: It's all in front of us?

xc: It's in front of me, anyway. Even if it can't become my spiritual background, it does offer me many perspectives. When I look at an issue, I try to consider it from a number of perspectives—historical, factual, cultural, economic, military— knowing I'll never be able to write lyric poems again as I've lost the ability to be purely lyrical. Of course, for some people that's all poetry ever is, but for me poetry is the writing of the Warring States masters. This is the essential difference between me and those people who may write a few poems but don't know much about poetry. I'm on another path. And if that's the path you've chosen, then you have to accept it. You can't expect everyone to nod their heads and recite your poetry, to chant your lines onstage, or to console themselves and their friends with your words. I don't mean to criticize anyone, I'm just taking a step back and saying I don't have the capacity for that sort of lyricism, don't have the ability. I only had it in the eighties.

xz: To put it bluntly, were the '80s a decade of lyricism?

xc: The '80s were definitely a lyrical decade overwhelmed by slogans. Whatever side you were on, you expressed yourself with slogans. But now we know that our problems can't be solved by slogans.

xz: So what do you think defines this decade?

xc: I don't have a good analogy for it, at least not right now.

xz: I'm worried about wasting the era, too. Sometimes I feel like we're living in a time without any nutritional value, with too much noise. But then sometimes, like you say, I wonder, "How do you turn it into something new?" Is this era of ours simply a nadir of creativity? Maybe everyone with creativity has gone the way of Mark Zuckerberg, into Facebook and Google?

xc: I have to say, though, agree that social media and technology requires creativity, too. You can't say there's no creativity in this era, which is really full of creativity. It's just that much of our creativity has shifted from literature into other areas.

And when it turns in that direction, it has to face another issue: obsolescence. And how long it takes to make that turn is itself an issue. I don't deny that various professions are full of creativity in our era, but at the risk of being pretentious (I've been speaking pretentiously all day): What does this kind of creativity have to do with civilization? China is a civilization—you can't get rid of the word, and if you care about the word "civilization," well, please answer me: What responsibility do you have for civilization? Are you responsible for success, for making money, for building buildings, or for all of it? If you say, "Live each day as your last, there's no tomorrow, civilization has nothing to do with me," well, I say, "Okay, so be it, you go your way and I'll go mine." But if you're even a little bit serious about the issue, and maybe would like to dive into "national education" after you've made your fortune, well then we can sit down and talk about it. What is your relationship to civilization?

xz: Is the sun going down? Let's talk until the sun's gone down!

xc: It happens to me a lot, that I sit down someplace and before long realize it's gotten dark.

xz: Has your sense of time changed much?

xc: There are many kinds of time—natural time, historical time, personal time. . . . You could say there are two types of artists: one type who works for eternity, and another type who doesn't. I used to be the kind who worked for eternity, but now I don't—or, to put it another way, you can't just be eternal simply because you want to be. To be eternal is a reward, and if we look back at literature from the past, such as Tang poetry, a lot of the poems collected in the *Complete Tang Poems* weren't written to last forever. They were written for an occasion, composed for a meal, or written to bid someone farewell.

xz: Or to pick up a woman in a brothel.

xc: Certainly. For instance, the quatrain by Cui Hu [772– 846], "One year ago today behind these doors / a face and a peach blossom reflected the other's red. / I do not know where that face has gone, / but the peach blossom still smiles in the spring breeze." This poem is immortal, but that immortality wasn't in the mind of the poet! For a lot of artists this is a threshold, so if they're starting out as poets, or as authors, or as visual artists, they'll leap past the first threshold and say, *I want to be like such-and-such a writer*. But beyond the threshold, you find that there's no point in wanting to be an excellent artist. For instance, Roberto Bolaño could be a poet at any place and any time—the second he found himself in communion with a poem in his mind, poetry would be born. I don't write like that.

None of the artists we call immortal are from our own era. We have figures who wither into immortality. The word "wither"—Yeats said, "Now may I wither into the truth." How do you acquire the truth? You wither into it. I wrote an essay about how Czesław Miłosz wasn't a master when he was alive, he was just one important poet. Miłosz had a million ties to the world around him—his friends, his relatives, his admirers, detractors, critics, defenders, but a few years after he died, he withered into a classic. While he was writing, he wasn't a classic. Time passed and I cast off this yoke.

xz: So your spectral readers, then, have you forgotten them?

xc: My spectral readers all embraced their own decaying eras. Of course, their ages decayed a little less quickly than ours, as things didn't fall into obsolescence as quickly. In the agricultural societies of the past, when you went out, you'd walk or else ride a horse or a donkey, while today we move at the speed of a train or a plane—there's no comparison.

xz: How do you maintain your own vitality? When you're young maybe it's natural, but after so much learning and experience, doesn't it get more difficult?

xc: Nietzsche—or maybe it was someone else!—said you only need to discover twenty-four truths each day to sleep well at night. We don't need to be so tough: if we can strive for one discovery like that each week, we won't feel like we've lived in vain. It takes perseverance to maintain a sense of discovery toward life, not to mention a free state of mind. Of course, as I say this, I'm aware it's not so easy as we might not be able to sustain a free state of mind—more often than not we get tangled up in something without even realizing it. But if we try, we might be able to step out of this framework, keep making discoveries about other people and about ourselves. Gabriel García Márquez once said something really beautiful when someone asked him what the reward was for him as a writer. He said that the greatest reward of writing is that a mind conditioned to write can immediately recognize another mind that has been conditioned to write. And so wherever you travel in the world, if you meet another writer you'll know them immediately— and anyone who is able to spot this skill in others will have at least a little bit of awareness of themselves, as well.

xz: I've got to be honest with you, in my last twenty years of reading, I think you are the person I resonate most with, in the core of my being.

xc: Thank you.

xz: I really feel like I understand all the things you're talking about, and you express all the things I want to say, about the present, about ourselves . . . it's like I'm listening to a wiser version of myself!

xc: I suddenly have this feeling that—not to be a mutual admiration society—I feel like the two of us are plural. There are four of us talking here.

xz: This feeling is quite strong.

xc: Thank you, thank you!

xz: It may have something to do with the similarity of our backgrounds, the tradition of pure reading, our hunger for experience, our desire for knowledge and to become moral individuals—all mixed together. But I haven't been as willing to cast off the rules of the '90s as you are. I still want to write something as good as Miłosz. I still have that strong desire.

xc: Each of us must undergo a kind of shedding-of-the-skin process, a switching-out-your-bones. I experienced that between 1989 and '92, and I still remember how excruciating that felt. There's no need for me to follow that direction anymore. I used to want to be a sage, but then I realized I was a Bull Demon King—that's how it feels. It may not have been your goal, but it's where you've ended up. . . . And it's pretty nice, sitting here in the dark. Maurice Maeterlinck said, "We do not know each other yet . . . because we have not yet dared to be silent together" [Alfred Sutro, trans.]. So even if we don't speak, just sitting here would be very good.

xz: So fitting for China today. Everyone is so noisy because no one really knows each other that well. We don't dare to be silent together.

xc: All hustle and bustle and everyone's a stranger.

xz: Seven or eight years ago I published a book called *The Homeland Stranger*. This time we can call it *The Decaying Strangers*.

xc: Don't say "decaying," say two people unafraid of obsolescence.

xz: Yes.

xc: I'm not afraid of being obsolete. If I'm obsolete then I'm obsolete. . . . We've sat out the day. It's gotten dark.

XI CHUAN 西川, born in Xuzhou, Jiangsu province, in 1963 and raised in Beijing, is one of China's most celebrated poets, essayists, and literary translators. Among the numerous prizes and honors he has received are the national Lu Xun Prize for Literature in China, the Cikada Prize for poetry in Sweden, and the Tokyo Poetry Prize in Japan. He formerly taught classical and modern Chinese literature at the Central Academy of Fine Arts, and is now a professor at the International Writing Center at Beijing Normal University. New Directions also published his collection *Notes on the Mosquito: Selected Poems*.

LUCAS KLEIN is a father, writer, and translator, and an associate professor of Chinese at Arizona State University. In addition to Xi Chuan he has translated contemporary Chinese poets Mang Ke and Duo Duo as well as medieval Chinese poet Li Shangyin.